THE ART OF FOLLOWING

BIBLICAL INSIGHTS FOR A NEW GENERATION OF MINISTRY

By:
Rev. Gene Herndon

"The Word is Eternal" Isaiah 40:8

Printed in the United States of America

Published by Aion Multimedia
20118 N 67th Ave
Suite 300-446
Glendale AZ 85308
www.aionmultimedia.com

ärt : skill acquired by experience, study, or observation

FOREWORD

In Luke 6:39-42, the very first question that is asked by Jesus is "Can the blind lead the blind? Shall they not both fall into a ditch?" The Holy Ghost asked me a question in regards to this verse. Can the blind lead the blind? I initially said no, but how do they both end up in the ditch? So the blind can lead the blind.

Luke 6:40 says, "the disciple is not above his master. The student will be like the teacher." To paraphrase; the student will see things like the teacher.

In this book, The Art of Following, my spiritual son, Pastor Gene Herndon, brings light and clarity to the Biblical principle of following- It is very important to whom you submit your life and ministry to.

The Art of Following is not man or hero worship. Jesus Christ is our Lord and Savior, but The Art of Following has many benefits. There is instruction, explanation, safety and help from someone who knows the things of the Spirit and things even in the natural. Through their teaching and guidance, one does not end up in the ditch.

Rev Ricky Edwards

Ricky Edwards Ministries

TABLE OF CONTENTS

Chapter One:
Art of Being Chosen

"For many are called, but few are chosen."
- Matthew 22:14

I received an email message not too long ago asking me this question:

"I know I'm called, but I don't know how to figure out what God wants from me, but I know I have a ministry. How do I go about getting into ministry?"

It was interesting because I think that a lot of people ask that question. In fact, that just might be one of the most commonly asked questions I hear. I have to admit though; it can be slightly agitating because when I give an answer, people tend to do the exact opposite of what I said. I think, at times, it is more of a wish than a true desire to be in ministry. The idea sounds better than the reality. I thought about this question, and realized it is not clear how to get into ministry, or how the process functions and how it works. I decided to write this book on how to get into ministry because I don't know that there is anything in circulation that explains it in detail. I know there are

1

several books that touch on various aspects of it, but I don't know if there's one that handles the very issue itself.

In the twelve years of the church I came up in, eight of those years I served under my pastor. I went where he went, and I traveled where he traveled at my own expense. I took care of all the arrangements; I carried his bag, and I carried his bible, Not that he could not do it himself (he was an ex boxer), I honored him and understood that if I wanted his anointing, it's not *taught*, it's *caught*. The anointing is only transferred through association, environment and influence. So when I realized that, I kept very close to him When I had to be corrected, I took the correction. When he told me what the vision was, I made sure I did his vision. What he said, whatever God told him to do, I did.

In twelve years of that ministry, I don't know (to the date of writing this book) if anybody has started a ministry for God. To my knowledge, there are only two people that have started a ministry and are still operating it today, and one of them was a pastor when I first attended services. There was only one other person that came out of twelve years of ministry who successfully started a ministry, and you're reading his book.

I began to think "Wait a minute, why do I clearly understand how this process works and why do I always seem to discern those who will make it, and those who I'm not sure will?" Undoubtedly, God put something in me. It's not a matter of patting myself on the back. Honestly anything good that is seen in me is God and anything that's wrong with me is me. It's just that simple.

Matthew 22:14 out of the Amplified says, "For many are called, (invited or summoned) but few are chosen."

This applies not only to salvation, but also, it is a unilateral concept that applies to ministry. Why do some make it, and some don't? Why do some become successful, and some don't? Why do

2

some fail, and why do some make it? The reason why few are chosen is because they cannot make it to their destination.

In Matthew 14, Peter had enough faith to get out of the boat. That's not to be mocked or diminished because Peter had more faith than anyone else in the boat. Sometimes, that's taught in a way where people knock Peter as if he was a man of weak faith. The reality is none of us would step out of the boat thinking we can walk on water. He did have some faith, but he just didn't have enough.

Faith is not all that is necessary; you also need character. Your calling (the anointing) will open doors- a man's gift makes room for him- but the anointing will open the door, bring you before kings, and character will keep you there. People say, "adversity builds character." That's a lie- an absolute falsehood. Adversity does not build character, adversity *reveals* it. Let all the problems come about, let disagreement set in, let people contend with one another. You will then see where people stand. We know that many are called and few are chosen, but what prevents people from walking in the anointing that God has for them?

I once met a man who told me I was supposed to be his spiritual father. I tried everything I could to convince him otherwise because he was flaky and did not keep true to his word. You can't be in ministry and be a flake. You must possess the ability to remain consistent because faithfulness is the number one requirement for ministry. Not full of faith, but faithful. People can have faith and not be faithful.

To be *faithful* is when you're the first to arrive and the last to leave. *Faithful* is when you say "I will do whatever is necessary to make it work." People do not want to make that commitment r because they have a fear of being abused. However, imagine if your child looked at you and said, "You know, I'm not going to do what you tell me to. I'm not sure if you're going to abuse me or not."

We can recognize and understand from a parental perspective how crazy that is, but yet and still it's a hindrance to people in the ministry. There is not one person in the Bible who was successfully launched into ministry and did not have somebody to help them. John the Baptist had a Jesus run-in before he even left the womb. There is a required process of development in order for God to birth the ministry that's in you. It is not God's desire that only few would be chosen; He wants all to be chosen. What people do not understand is that there is a difference between your divine calling and your divine assignment. Your assignments are not always given in the area of your calling.

When you're going to school, you're given homework assignments, and the succession of completed assignments gives you good grades. You eventually receive a degree, but there are a series of homework assignments that build up to your degree. Likewise, there are also a series of assignments that prepare you for your calling. People will say things such as, "I'm not called to sweep the floor." You're not called to sweep the floor; you're assigned to sweep the floor. In your assignment, you will find the development of your character. If your immediate reaction is, "I don't want to do that and I'm not called to do that!" You are not ready. What are you going to do when God assigns you to do something that you feel is not your calling?

"How do you get into ministry?" Here's my answer. I typed an e-mail response and I said:

"Here's how you get into ministry. First, find a church that will feed you. Once you find that church, show up. Show up if they have Sunday or Wednesday service. Demonstrate faithfulness. Then once you start becoming faithful, tithe to it. Show that you support them. Then, get involved in ministry wherever there's a need. Start serving in the area of the need, you will develop in your gift, and eventually you will walk in your calling."

People begin to wonder, "What is my calling?" So they only want to participate in activities that they feel are in line with what they're called to do rather than what they need to do. What you are required to do may not, in your mind, have anything to do with your calling. In the assignment, there are things that God is working out of you. If your attitude needs improvement, He's going to place you around people that will agitate you. While you're complaining, "Oh, these people…" The day you stop grumbling is when your ready for a new assignment.

Our society is so rebellious nowadays. If they do not like what they're asked to do, they will take off and do whatever they want to without recognizing that the call of God is on their life. One time, a guy came to me, angry with his pastor because he hadn't recognized the gift that was in the man, and he wanted to attend the church I pastor. I said, "Don't you even think about it. You go back to your pastor and apologize to him. You need to submit, and you stay submitted. If he tells you to sweep the floor, sweep the floor." That's how this process works. Do I need more people at the church? Absolutely, but I know what is appropriate and what is not. If he recognized where his supply came from, he would know he needed to stay, to respect, honor and serve at his pastor's direction.

"Why are few chosen?" Well, I'm going to endeavor to answer that question. If there are areas in which you need to make an adjustment, you have two choices. One, you can get mad, and say, "This guy is crazy!" That's fine with me. Just do me a favor, find somebody who's not crazy and then apply everything I just shared with you. Alternatively, you can think "Maybe there's some areas I need to make some changes in," and just make the adjustments. I don't think people understand how close we are to seeing the coming of Christ. We don't have time for strife, we don't have time for bickering or for problems and nonsense and the stupidity that we're constantly seeing. This is a race to find as many souls as possible and bring them to the

Lord. That's what this is all about. We need to understand how to keep the main thing, the main thing.

"They said it wouldn't be right for us to abandon our responsibilities for preaching and teaching the word of God to help care for the poor. So friends, choose seven men among you whom everyone trusts, men full of the Holy Spirit and good sense and we'll assign them this task. Meanwhile, we'll stick to our assigned tasks of prayer and speaking God's word. The congregation thought this was a great idea."
-Acts 6:3-5 MSG

In this passage, the leaders explained to the people that they desired to continue preaching, teaching, and studying the word so that everyone would be fed.. They needed the congregation to do all the other functions of the ministry. So the leadership requested a search for seven people of honest report and good sense(It's brilliant, wish I'd have thought of it). Then the congregation said, "That's a great idea!"

"The congregation thought this was a great idea. They went ahead and chose- Stephen, a man full of faith and the Holy Spirit, Philip, Procorus, Nicanor, Timon, Parmenas, Nicolas, a convert from Antioch. Then they presented them to the apostles. Praying, the apostles laid on hands and commissioned them for their task."
Acts 6:5-6 MSG

Your gifts are developed within the local church. You don't serve in one church and then jump around from church to church in attempts to seek out the ones who will recognize and use your gift. In the secular world, a woman who goes around from man to man to discover who will recognize her gift would be called names that we will not include here. The gift is to be brought to the local church where you'll be developed. If you don't believe that, then find a place where you'll be fed and stay there. I assure you, if you don't remain in one place, it will confuse your spirit. An inconsistent diet of doctrine can bring confusion in the same way eating all kinds of different foods can agitate your stomach.

Some of the books people read are doctrinally unhealthy. They will present their "new found" information to their pastor, and if it's not scriptural, they will confuse their spirit. They're not thinking correctly. This is what I do when someone comes to me:

I'll say, "Well, tell me scripturally why that's true."

"Well, the book says… "

"No, no, don't tell me what that book says."

Every book I read goes back to the *Analogy of Faith*. The *Analogy of Faith* is "scripture always interprets scripture". We cannot have truthful interpretations without scripture.

The stoning of Stephen (Acts:7) was an instrumental part in the course of events that brought the Apostle Paul (who wrote two-thirds of the New Testament) to salvation in Christ. Stephen started out waiting on tables and feeding the poor. That was his assignment; it wasn't his calling. Philip was called to be an Evangelist, so why was he serving tables? That was his assignment.

They, the pastors, couldn't leave what was important. I tell people all the time, "Don't let the increase distract you from what is important. Keep the main thing, the main thing." The increase was brought about by the leaderships prayer, study, and preaching." We need people who understand their assignment is designed to develop them into what God has called them to be. Understand, your assignment, may have nothing to do, in your mind, with what you were called to do. However, since society has bred a microwave generation that says, "I want it all, and I want it now", they do not recognize the necessity for the development.

There's a difference between being called and being chosen. *Chosen* means you are now separated for the work.

"I think I'm called." Great!

"Shouldn't I...?" No!

"But I'm called." Yes, but you haven't been chosen yet.

You are only chosen after you have been prepared. When I want counsel, I go to people who have been pastors; people who understand the drama I go through myself. I need people who know how to conquer the demonic craziness that I wrestle with and understand how to deal with the insane things that come at me on a regular basis. I don't seek advice from the congregation. They won't have a clue what I'm going through, not even a little bit. They will, however, love to judge the situation. I approach the people that understand. They've seen it before; they have higher levels of revelation and I recognize their authority in my life.

I'll let you in on a little secret. I consult the Holy Ghost first, and my mentors second, for every major decision I've ever made in my life. I tend not to make decisions without asking them first. Whatever I do is a reflection of what they've told me to do; regardless of whether I agreed or liked it, or whether it made me comfortable or uncomfortable. Now you would think, "Why does he have such trust?" They've never been wrong -and more importantly, even if my mentors were to be wrong, I know they had my best interest at heart. You do not submit to someone you cannot trust. If you do not trust them, move on and find someone else. They will make mistakes; they're human. Adam walked with God in the cool of the day and he still messed up. Don't keep your eyes on the man because you'll lose track of what God is doing in the world. People can be disappointing, but if you know their heart toward you then you know that they never meant to do you wrong. However, the first thing that Satan will try to do is disconnect you from your supply.

The apostles laid hands on the seven men and commissioned them for their task. Do you know how many people run around proclaiming what God told them to do privately and it has no scriptural support?There is only one answer for that .... "No, He didn't!"

God will speak and confirm information through your leadership until you are in leadership. I don't mean leadership in the church- I mean the Five Fold Offices. You can be a leader in the church while you are still a sheep. There's only one pastor.

I love what I do to be honest with you. Yet despite all the challenges, you want to know what really gets me excited? Watching the people as they change, and when I listen to them talk I remember what they were like only a year before. I honestly believe that I have a mandate to make sure that people will fulfill the plan of God for their lives. I really do believe that. However, just because their phone rings and they feel they have been called does not mean they have received marching orders yet.

The apostles commissioned the seven men for their tasks. The Word of God spread and the number of disciples in Jerusalem increased dramatically. That began to create synergy. *Synergy* is defined as "the increased effectiveness that results when two or more people or businesses work together". One plus one no longer makes two, but it produces four, five, six, seven...etc. The outcome is more than what the two alone could have created by themselves; that's synergy. When the people finally got it through their heads and said, "We have a need, people need to be fed. Let's get seven men of honest report, lay hands on them, and commission them for the task" they got more people involved in the right position, in the right place,and with the right task assigned to them. Then, they began to prosper and the number of disciples grew dramatically.

What if they had said, "We'll stop studying to serve tables instead"? All of a sudden the message suffers.. When they need to flow in the Holy Ghost, it becomes more difficult to hear Him because they're exhausted.

If you feel that you're in the church where you're supposed to be, your calling will never be developed outside of the auspices of that church. Whoever that pastor is, he or she is the one who will be responsible for your development.

I always feel a certain level of uneasiness saying these things because I wonder "what if people say that's just self-serving?" This is for your benefit. People who struggle usually come up with crazy ideas and plans that they should not act upon and then they wonder why it doesn't work out. Then, they ask, "What happened? I thought I was called." You are called; you just haven't been chosen yet- and you can't choose yourself.

When I was a teenager I used to work in retail at the mall. On my lunch break, I would go out, sit in the mall and watch people. It always intrigued me to put their stories together. I am the consummate student- always questioning and pondering. I have studied and studied within myself, "Why, when I was with my pastor, was I not afraid of getting hurt even though he made decisions I didn't like and did things I didn't agree with?" Interestingly enough, they always worked out for him. I just learned not to put my foot in my mouth anymore and waited to see what happened. But I always wondered to myself "Why did I have such trust in him to the point where I was never afraid that he would do me wrong even if he did something wrong, even if he made a mistake?" Then I began to realize that I trusted God more than I trusted him, and what I realized is that sometimes people will put more faith in the individual, than they will in God. When an individual has a problem, they lose their salvation figuratively over it because they were not really trusting God. If you trust God, then you know that no weapon formed against you will ever prosper and you know that no time is wasted time. Even the things that my pastor made mistakes in, I learned to handle those situations differently. So no time was lost time, and when I would think about it, I said "Why didn't I ever think he was taking advantage of me?"

In one year, I gave $33,000 in tithe. I wasn't worrying about, "Is that a lot of money, is that not a lot of money?" I trusted God and I knew where He had placed me. If I knew where God placed me, then he placed me there for a reason whether I knew it or not. My ability to submit allowed me to grow. Sometimes I think to myself, "How crazy is it that I'm the only one out of that ministry to start a work in twelve years?" But you know how many people looked at me and said, "Are you the pastor's pet?" Sure. "Well, you're just a yes-man." You're right, whatever he says. "Yes sir!" It's a curious thing that the world begins to twist that into a way that almost makes you feel like you've lost some part of yourself in order to be submitted. Jesus said, "The things you see me do is because I see my father do it." We understand Jesus' submission to God, but did you ever stop and think that God the Father is God, but so was Jesus? If anybody had the right to say, "I don't want to be submitted", it would have been him. How does someone submit to themselves? It's in the submission aspect that people become lost. If I ask you to do something unethical, immoral or illegal, don't do it.If it's not any of those three things, there's a lack of submission when you don't understand what you're told to do.

God doesn't operate through committees. Moses did not have a committee. Jesus did not have a committee. Paul did not have a committee. You can research from the front to the back of the Bible if you want, but they didn't have committees. They were men who were appointed and anointed of God and called for a task. In that task, they were accountable, but they did not have "The Light Committee".

"We need some new lights in the sanctuary, let's form a committee."
"Well, I think we should buy GE Lights."
"Well, I think we should buy..."

The church has become, so committee oriented that nothing gets done.

It's the responsibility of the house to develop those that are in it. Some of you don't see your development process, so you think you have to go elsewhere. That's the bait of Satan. How could you go serve somewhere else and know there's a need in your own house? If I were talking about your home, you wouldn't take food to somebody else's house and let your own children starve.

Some people won't attend church unless they have something to do there. If they're not on a schedule, they won't show up. There's no demonstration of faithfulness or commitment, and then they wonder why, when they volunteer to help, I don't say anything. When the chips are down, I need to know they're ready. How can we fight a war if they're on vacation? I choose my battle mates very carefully because I need to know that when we go to war, I don't need to be searching for them.

It's amazing how many people offer their service but don't recognize their inconsistent behavior and lack of faithfulness. They wonder why I'm not moved. I'm waiting to see the bare bones- the basics of what is required to be in ministry. I don't have a choice not to show up to the church. The congregation would be mad if I didn't show up. "Who does he think he is? He's the shepherd!" Well, they're the sheep, and you can't have a shepherd without sheep.

"God and Jesus and the angels all back me up in these instructions. Carry them out without favoritism, without taking sides. Don't appoint people to church leadership positions too hastily. If a person is involved in some serious sins, you don't want to become an unwitting accomplice."
1 Timothy 5:21-22 MSG

If you mess up, your leader is the one held responsible. Some of you are participating in activities that are not sanctioned by the church. The leadership is not responsible for that, and if it goes south, your causing problems in the body and you are on your own. I knew that submitting to my pastor protected me. I knew that there were things that kept me safe because I was under the shepherd's rod. He was looking out for wolves and he could see them coming faster than I could. The sheep are at ground level, the shepherd's at sky level. That's why we stand upright; sheep are hunched over. My vision is better because I'm a shepherd. The anointing on my life causes me to see things that I don't always understand, but I see it.

I knew that my pastor was there for my protection, and he was there to help me. I knew he was there to keep me safe and to keep me from harm. He was there to keep me from myself. Some of you desperately want to be in ministry, but you don't know the challenges for which you're asking. You don't even know about the fight you've asked to be in or the demonic things you're about to encounter. You just want to be behind the pulpit. You better wake up! I'm not trying to discourage you from ministry; I'm trying to help you see the reality of it. If you think the pastor's expectations are ridiculous, let me tell you something. The auspicious one in which I serve has higher expectations than me. If you can't submit to the man you can see, then you won't be able to submit to the God you can't see.

The Bible tells us not to lay hands on anyone suddenly (1 Timothy 5). It had taken David fifteen years, Paul fourteen years, Moses forty years, and Elisha twenty years- before they were chosen. What took so long, and why do we expect to have it so quickly? I spent eight years serving my pastor. If he went away, I went with him at my own expense because I understood that the anointing is not taught, it's caught. The anointing was transferred through my service, not through my words. Someone was sharing a story with me about a person they knew. Evidently, this person did something that they believed God instructed them to do, but they did it outside of the auspices of the church. As a result, there were problems that should not have occurred. I thought to myself, "This is why people should not try to go before they're ready." When they are ready, they will go with the authority of the organization that sent them. However, when people are not submitted, then they are not protected. I began to wonder, "How many people understand that there's protection that comes with remaining under the cover?"

The basis of the Jezebel spirit is to refuse leadership, submission and headship. Most guys will say, "Well, that's a woman." That's not true. The spirit of Jezebel was on Judas. I've heard guys say, "Yeah my wife's a Jezebel." So you know the first thing I say, "That makes you an Ahab." You permit it; it'll happen.

Gehazi went out and told Naaman he wanted to collect the money that Elisha didn't want.(2 Kings 5). It is not wrong for a minister to receive an offering, so technically Elisha could have taken it, but he said, "No, I don't want to. This guy initially came with the wrong attitude and the wrong heart. I'm not taking anything he has." However, Gehazi decided, "Hey, since Elisha doesn't want it, I'll take it." Technically, was he wrong? He didn't violate the mandates of God, but he undermined his leadership.When Gehazi returned, the first thing Elisha said was, "Didn't my spirit go with you?"

"Hey, what'd you do?"

"Nothing."

"Where you been?"

"Nowhere."

That question was asked to let Gehazi know that Elisha saw where he went, because he was operating on a borrowed anointing. Here's an example of a borrowed anointing. In the church, we teach people different things and get them involved in ministry. Maybe we send them to a homeless shelter and the power of God falls. When they start ministering, they love the feeling and then they think, "Maybe that's my anointing." It's not, they're functioning on a borrowed anointing. The anointing that's on the ministry or the Man/Woman of God will come off on you to do a task or a purpose. That's why they laid hands on the seven men. The leaders would not need to lay hands on each person if they already had the anointing.

"As they ministered to the Lord, and fasted, the Holy Ghost said, Separate me Barnabas and Saul for the work whereunto I have called them."
Acts 13:2

The Holy Ghost was speaking. Now, if the Holy Ghost spoke through Barnabas and Saul, wouldn't they have said, "Separate *us*?" The Holy Ghost said, "Separate these two individuals" through someone else. They were together fasting and praying with the leadership. "To which I have called them," means they have been called and they are now chosen.

It is important to recognize that your leaders decide when you're ready. If you are not selected by your leadership, you tend to want to move in other directions to fulfill a need that you feel you have. You're not being deprived; you're being protected from circumstances, and sometimes from yourself.

None of you can cast the first stone, not one of you. We all have personal challenges, problems and issues. But it's a different matter when you do something that God told you to do. If God didn't tell me to be a prophet, but I know how to prophesy, then I should not be trying to act in the office of a prophet. I can use *the gift* of prophesy; I can bless and help people,, but that is not what God called me to do. So, while I'm over here "doing good" whatever God asked me to do is not being accomplished and I'm actually *doing damage*.

A lot of people seek to "do good", but they don't recognize that they're causing damage. They think "doing good" is doing God. Doing "good" is not doing God. Whatever God instructed you to do is what you're supposed to do. When you're faithful and committed, God does not reveal it to you only, he also reveals it to your leadership.

Satan is extremely crafty. He'll put a plan together that seems good. The Bible says the ways unto a man may seem right, but that doesn't mean it's God (Proverbs 21). You can do good and not do God. You can be in places where you shouldn't be and it may feel good to you, but it might not be God.

In regards to the email I discussed at the beginning of this chapter, I responded with the answer to her question. She replied with, "I guess I just thought you were going to tell me the answer." That's how Satan blinds people. I gave her the answer. She saw the answer, she read it and then responded, "I thought you were going to give me the answer." You have to recognize how God leads, how He works, and how He leads through headship.

If we are to be honest, this is one of the reasons why families fall apart. You have a husband who doesn't know he's in charge and is responsible for his family. He lets everyone do what they want to do and the family moves out from his covering. You have a wife who doesn't want to submit to her husband and now she's out from under the covering. Then, we wonder why families are struggling and dysfunction abounds.

God has an order for the family unit. Woman was taken from the womb of man. A man gave birth to a woman; the woman gave birth to children. There is an order of headship in the domestic family. There's also an order of headship in the spiritual family, and it follows rank. It is unscriptural and unbiblical for a wife to be telling her husband what to do and how to do it in a rebellious manner. Does that mean he gets to be a jerk? Absolutely not, he has the responsibility to love his family like Christ loves the church. If Christ loved the church and gave His life for it, then husbands are supposed to give his life for the family.

There's a rank and order for spiritual things- God is the Father and Jesus was called the Chief Shepherd. That means there are under-shepherds. There is a line of order that comes with authority. People wonder why they don't feel the power of God in their life and it's because they're not submitted to the line of authority. If you submit to the power, you receive the power.

People wonder, "Why's the family all messed up?" It's completely out of order. In society, men are relegated to idiots who can't do anything. On every television show, he's a bumbling fool. I beg to differ because I know Christian men who are not idiots. They have the Holy Ghost inside of them. They are not weak, and they are not stupid. If they have the Holy Ghost then they can learn all things and know all things. We have been raising children that have no respect for authority. They respect power, but power is not always seen whereas authority is always known. When you're under authority, you're meek and teachable. You hear the instruction and you apply it. If I say, "I want to meet with you", if I put my time into you in any way, shape or form it is because I see something valuable in you. I don't have time to waste. I pick and choose where I put my time. If I spend my time on the phone or in person, I am not wasting; I'm investing because I believe in you. If you do not catch on, I will not spend my time on you. I do not have all the time in the world. I have to seek those that are willing to be faithful, willing to submit, to trust, to love, and be looking out for my best interests as I look out for theirs. It's that simple. If you want to be in ministry, I suggest you read what I'm saying and take it to heart.

The Bible says you will give an account for every useless word you speak (Matthew 12). When you look up that word *useless* it means "to lack power", or basically anything that wasn't God. God said,

"They will come to me, and they'll say, 'Lord, Lord we did miracles in your name"? His response was "Depart from me you worker of iniquity, I never knew you." They did "good", but they weren't doing *God*.

I have watched people come into the ministry. When the anointing starts to bring power into their lives, they will become strong and confident while doing the things of God. Then, they get offended, walk away, and spend the rest of their lives trying to fill the void and figure out why they can't move forward. It's simply because they've abandoned their position and lost the power that the anointing brings. No matter how many times I preach it, they leave with, "Well, that was a great message. I sure wish he'd give me the answer." I just did!

Be wise enough to see it. Be wise enough to recognize that I'm not teaching this because I somehow feel this is just for me. I'm doing this because I believe there are not enough Word and Spirit churches in the world. Too few institutions are reaching out into the world and doing something to make a difference. I firmly believe that if the body of believers would come together (without the strife, the nonsense, and the garbage) and say, "You know what? We're going to stick together like glue and do what God has called us to do," we can make a difference. We can turn our cities upside down. I believe we could place the church universal in a position to make a difference. When people have needs, they're not going to think, "Can I go to the government?" They're going to think, "Wait a minute: there's that church over there. I can get food and clothes from that place." I am talking about empowerment on a completely different level, but one person cannot do it alone. If I could do it on my own, I promise you I would have.

"Well, I know I'm called, I wish he'd just give me the answer."

How long does it take? I don't know. Your time is not based on me; it's based on you. Some of you are missing your assignments. That's why you're not graduating with your degree.

Chapter Two:
The Art of Preparation

I'm learning that every time there is a significant move of God there will always be absurdity from Satan that goes along with it. People tend to lose their minds and forget who they are in those moments, but Satan cannot schedule your destruction, he can only schedule your distraction. What he tends to do is construct such an elaborate scheme that people don't understand why they're offended, they don't understand why they're struggling and it truly is just a spiritual attack. If you're going to be smack dabbed in the middle of Satan's plan, make sure that you are following God's plan to disrupt Satan "Many are invited (or summoned), but few are chosen." Matthew 22:14 AMP

As time is getting closer to our Savior's return, I'm starting to see that people don't necessarily understand the process of fulfilling their call. You can receive the invitation, but not all are actually chosen out of those that are invited. People can mistake the invitation (the call) for full authorization to engage in what it was that God has called them to. Just because you have received the call, doesn't mean that it's the right time to move. There's a time between receiving the call and what we know as "being separated", and that time is called *preparation*, where God is getting you prepared. He's placing you in situations to condition your character, to adjust your attitude, and to see if you can stick with it.

It's amazing to me that shortly before I'm about to promote someone or use them in the ministry, they do something to disqualify themselves. It rarely fails. That demonstrates they're not ready yet. I don't hold it against them; I'm not mad at them- I'm slightly disappointed if I can be honest- but the reality is I just know they're not ready. It's similar to baking a piece of chicken. You pull it out of the oven and if it's still pink in the middle, you push it back in and wait. It's bizarre because most people do not know that the moment they give up is just before they're about to be promoted.

It's a challenge, because sometimes you have to move by faith. Faith requires you to lead a lifestyle that is not dependent upon what you see in the world, but what you believe in your heart. It is exceptionally difficult to get people to live by faith, but the truth of the matter is God *expects* you to live by faith. Faith will never leave you ashamed, faith will never disappoint you, and faith will never let you fail. Faith will never forsake you; the God type of faith cannot fail. It's just not possible. Some say, "Well I was in faith and it failed." Then you weren't in faith. What you were in was called "hope". *Hope* and *faith* are not the same. *Hope* is a beautiful thing and it's a partner to your faith, but when you are in faith it goes beyond hope. Faith is a dispensation of expectancy that moves beyond the realm of hoping and wishing. It moves into a place where you receive that which you know belongs to you. You receive it; you have it and no one can convince you otherwise, despite what you may see, think, or feel.
"Well, I'm in faith." Are you? If you are, then your faith will move mountains and change circumstances. If you are, your faith will shake the very foundations of the world - If you really are in faith.

"Then Jesus said unto them, Verily, verily , I say unto you, Except ye eat the flesh of the Son of man, and drink his blood, ye have no life in you. Whoso eateth my flesh, and drinketh my blood,

hath eternal life; and I will raise him up at the last day. For my flesh is meat indeed, and my blood is drink indeed. He that eateth my flesh, and drinketh my blood, dwelleth in me, and I in him. As the living Father hath sent me, and I live by the Father: so he that eateth me, even he shall live by me. This is that bread which came down from heaven not as your fathers did eat manna, and are dead: he that eateth of this bread shall live forever. These things said he in the synagogue, as he taught in Capernaum. Many therefore of his disciples, when they had heard this, said, This is an hard saying; who can hear it? When Jesus knew in himself that his disciples murmured at it, he said unto them, Doth this offend you?"
-John 6:53-61

In this passage, Jesus is explaining a divine revelation to the disciples. He's telling them, "You're going to eat the flesh of my flesh and drink the blood of my blood." We understand present day what he was explaining to them. He was telling them that they were going to partake of communion. Interestingly enough, they were offended. "This is a difficult thing to hear!"

Well, here's the problem. They were called, so now they're in the process of being prepared. They've come to the master; Jesus is training them up and he tells them "This is what you're going to have to do," and they get offended. The next question Jesus asked is, "Does this offend you?"

If you believe that you have a call of God on your life, there is only one way to handle that call; it's a biblical way. You will find no shortcut in the Bible that bypasses the training process necessary to prepare you for your life calling. Jesus is explaining to them what they have to do, but they never gave him the opportunity to expound on what he meant exactly. They just got offended, started murmuring and their familiarity produced great offense.

People who are familiar with you will become offended very quickly, because they assume too much of you. Familiarity assumes way too much. Next thing you know, while you're preaching, they're cracking jokes and drawing attention to themselves because they're too familiar with you. All of a sudden, they're talking to you, asking you questions, and they're in your life in a way that you never invited them to be. Then (the grand finale), they're judging your personal decisions..

Moses decided he was going to marry an Ethiopian woman, and Aaron and Miriam did not approve (Numbers 12). Let me rephrase that into today's language. Moses decided he was going to marry a little black girl and Aaron and Miriam said, "We don't like interracial relationships. We hear from God too! We don't think that's right!"
God called Miriam and Aaron and said, "Come on out here. Let me talk to you for a minute."

God said to them, "I speak to you in darkness of visions and dreams and in bits and pieces, but I speak to Moses mouth to mouth."
In other words, "Don't get it twisted to think that you have more revelation and understanding than the leader I put over you, because to him, I speak directly; to you, I give you bits." This is why in the local church there is no higher office than that of a shepherd. God said to Aaron and Miriam, "*If* there be a prophet among you..." There is an erroneous doctrine running around trying to make the case that the prophets and the apostles are in charge of all the churches. Notice, God made it clear that He speaks to the pastor mouth to mouth. Now, of course, everyone should have someone that they are submitted to. However, understand that God always works from the top going down, not vice versa. He used Jethro to bring correction to Moses, not those under Moses. What God was telling Aaron and Miriam, in essence, was not to grow familiar with their leader. Now the interesting thing is Aaron made the adjustment, but Miriam did not and she was struck with leprosy.

I'm not advising that you blindly follow the leadership because that's not what you do, but I can tell you this much. If you cannot go to the word of God and disprove what you're hearing, your best bet is to shut up and learn. I learned a long time ago (under my pastor) that I don't like the taste of shoe leather. I realized that my best bet was to keep my mouth shut until I knew better. Then, even the things I didn't understand eventually became clear if I was just patient enough to find out. It was always the ones who were quick to fly off the handle, who were not temperate, who could not control their emotions and rose up in the pastor's face that looked stupid. I don't like to look stupid; it's not my way, but those people are the ones who get offended and leave.

There were only 12 out of 70 disciples that thought if they had to cannibalize Jesus; they were going to do it. Twelve people made a decision to say, "Well, okay. Give me some barbecue sauce. If I have to do that, then that's the way it is." When Jesus said, "Hey Peter, are you going to leave me too"? Peter said, "Where we going to go? You're the one that has the answer to eternal life. There's nowhere else to go." But there were 58 people that found another place to go.

You can't go to just any church. You need to go to *the* church, the one that is for you, and the one where God has a supply for you. You need to be at the one that speaks right to your spirit and offends your soul. How do you find the place that speaks to your spirit and offends your soul?

What we have today is a majority of soul churches; churches that speak to the soul. They're playing secular music on the platform, and Pastor's inviting members to concerts. "Let's go see the latest pop artist performance!" They're catering to the soul, teaching you self-help methods, *"How To Have Your Best Life Yet!"* and *"Five Keys to Making Every Day Like Friday"*. They're speaking to your soul. You can't attend just any church; you must go where God has put you. The Bible tells us that God placed us in the body as it pleased him... not us!

Here's the beautiful part about it. If you would think of yourself as a plant, you will grow where you're planted.

Imagine if a plant in your house said to you, "I don't think I want to be here anymore. I'm going somewhere else." The same thing happens every day in the church. "Well, I don't know that I like this anymore. I just want to be told that it's okay. Why can't Pastor and I go see the latest pop artist? It just shows that the Pastor's cool!"

I am not here to "be cool" or win popularity contests. I'm here to help you save your soul for eternity. I could not care less about these other things that people are so concerned with. The deeper you go in the word, the less you become concerned with the nonsense of the world. You see everything in the world as a distraction rather than reality.

Fifty-eight people found somewhere else to go. Why? They became offended. I guarantee within that fifty-eight; there were ones that said, "Hey, Jesus allowed us to come and be with him. I've been with Jesus; I can go start my own ministry now! I don't have to do what he's asked me to do. I'm not eating his flesh and his blood! Let him force everybody else to do that. Doesn't he know who I am? I'm one of the original seventy!" We struggle with the same thing today. This is why people are unable to walk in the calling that God has for them.

Once again, this is why many are called, but few are chosen. There are times where you don't have the ability to discern higher levels of revelation that comes from mentors and those over you in the Lord; it's above your pay grade. That doesn't make it wrong; it just means it's above your level. Jesus had revelation; he shared it with the disciples, and their response was, "Yeah, well we're not fitting to do that." They start murmuring and complaining, and the beginning of all dissension starts with murmuring.

I remember in one of Tony Cooke's books; he talked about how he went to visit a lady from the church. He served under Kenneth Hagin Sr. for many years and was also the Dean of Rhema Bible College. He went to visit this lady in the hospital and she said, "Brother Cooke, thank you for coming to see me. I can't believe that Pastor Hagin wouldn't come see me."

Now, this is a perfect opportunity for him to say, "I know, he's just so busy, he's terrible.." and sell himself, but his response was, "Ma'am listen, I'm so grateful that God gave him the wisdom to know that he can't be everywhere at once. God gave him men and women of God, such as myself,who are willing to serve his vision and to be where he wants us to be. He personally asked me to come here and see you, to make sure that you were okay, and to tell you that he's praying for you and believing God for you."
He shut her down. Now, why?

When someone comes to you to murmur and complain against the organization in which you're in, you have to ask yourself, what did they see in you? Do they think that you're purchasable with their words, that you are not strong enough in mind to withstand the onslaught of their garbage? Why did they decide, "Well let me come to you and dump on you and see if I can sway you"? Did you ever stop and think, "Hey, wait a minute. Why did they come to me? What iniquity do they see in me that made them think that I could be bought so quickly?" These are things that sow division. It starts with murmuring.. "I can't believe Pastor asked me to do that, doesn't he know I'm anointed? Why do I have to do that? I think we should do this a different way." There's a place for people who want to do things their own way. It's just not the local church.

The reason being is because the pastor is responsible spiritually for each and every one of the souls in his congregation. Did you notice the Bible tells pastors to watch over the souls of the sheep? They don't watch over your spirit; your spirit belongs to God. They are watching over your mind, your will and your emotions. It is their responsibility to give an account for you. Do you think that they would relinquish responsibility to some haphazard person who doesn't understand spiritual things, and then have to answer for it? If I told you you're responsible for something and if you don't do it right you're going to die, believe me, when somebody comes to you and says, "Hey I want to do it this way." You're going to say, "Not on this watch! Wait until so-and-so comes, they're not afraid of death."

Of course, the consequences may not be as dire as death, but I'm afraid to disappoint the Father. In that, I have a responsibility as a shepherd of the house. I'm not the shepherd of every house just the one God gave to me. I'm not telling you this because I desire to be a control freak. I'm telling you this because I'm responsible. It's funny how when people see the responsible party; they do not respect the authority comes with the position, especially not over them. But if they're responsible, they want all the power that comes with the responsibility. Isn't that something?

I want to talk to you about a couple of different divine relationships. I want to show you something in the New Testament that I believe is very important. Acts 15:36-40, "And some days after Paul said unto Barnabas, Let us go again and visit our brethren in every city where we have preached the word of the Lord, and see how they do. And Barnabas determined to take with them John, whose surname was Mark. But Paul thought not good to take him with them, who departed from them from Pamphylia, and went not with them to the work. And the contention was so sharp between them, that they departed asunder one from the other: and so Barnabas took Mark, and sailed unto Cyprus; And Paul chose Silas, and departed, being recommended by the brethren unto the grace of God. And he went through Syria, and Cilicia, confirming the churches."

Barnabas and Paul were brought together for a divine relationship. Barnabas was the one who introduced Paul to the ministry. If you know the history of Paul, you know that he used to be named Saul of Tarsus, and Saul was killing and persecuting Christians. He had an experience on the Road of Damascus which turned his whole life around.Now, he's trying to get into ministry and nobody trusts him. This ought to help you understand just because people profess Christ does not mean that you instantly trust them. Sometimes, to gauge where they're at you need to test them against the Word.

God called Barnabas to come alongside Paul to help him gain entry into the ministry. The Holy Ghost said, "Separate me Paul and Barnabas for the work which to I've called them." Everybody trusted Barnabas, but they didn't know Paul. God created a divine relationship between them in order for the ministry to be successful. In the aforementioned scripture, Paul and Silas left upon the recommendation of the brethren and endorsed by the grace of God. It says that Barnabas and Mark just left, period.

Now, Paul said to Barnabas, "I don't want to take John Mark, he left us. He deserted us. When we needed him, he broke wide. At the first sign of trouble, he's gone. Now you want to take him with us again?" This is the last time you will hear Barnabas' name in the entire Bible. Barnabas was the one who introduced Paul, but Paul was the one who had the ministry. He did not recognize the given instruction when Paul said, "No", so he decided, "I'm going to do what I want to do," and he left with no grace of God, right off the pages of scripture. Why? He could not recognize his position in the ministry.

I served under my pastor for eight years. I carried his bags, went wherever he went. Wherever he preached, I was there. There were very few of his sermons that I did not hear over that eight-year period of time. I scheduled my vacations around his schedule, and I took care of my personal business. I ran three companies around his schedule because I understood that the anointing is not taught; it's caught. I understood that if I wanted the anointing that I need to be around the anointed. He taught it— hammered it, hammered it and hammered it— but I learned it and I understood.

Most of my understanding came from my personal conversations with him. He could preach the paint off the walls, don't get me wrong, but I learned the most when we would drive for 4 hours to wherever he was going to preach. I learned more sitting across the dinner table from him just listening than I did during his sermons. I understood that if he was the man with the ministry, I needed to recognize my position. I didn't think, "Well since I'm driving he'll go where I'm driving him to. If I'm paying for dinner, I'll take him where I want to go." Knowing this will keep you successful in the ministry, while failure to recognize it will get you to a place where you're constantly offended, and you'll lose your opportunities.

Barnabas left and here's the inept part about it. Later on the Apostle Paul said, "Bring me John Mark, for he is profitable unto me for the ministry." (2 Timothy 4) It wasn't that Paul was saying "Never", He said, "Not now." He had enough discernment to see that John Mark wasn't ready when Barnabas wanted to take him. How come Barnabas didn't see it?

"Oh, I wonder why Pastor doesn't make you the Assistant Pastor. If I was him..."

"You could preach like he can preach. I don't see why he doesn't have you teach when he..."

They don't know what their pastors know and they don't see what their pastor sees. Not that there's anything wrong with you, but it might not be the right time. Timing is everything, and Paul knew timing. Barnabas did not. Paul wrote three quarters of the New

Testament; Barnabas did not. Paul stayed on and still did mighty works for God, but we never hear from Barnabas ever again.

This is why ministries fail. People will not stay where they're assigned to be, they refuse to stay in line, and they will not submit to the training and development process.They will not submit to the oversight of their leadership. If I were Barnabas, I would have said, "Paul, we'll take whomever you want to take, just take me. As long as I have a seat, I don't care who else sits next to me." Tragically, Barnabas left the scriptures because he didn't understand that he wasn't the one *with* the ministry. He was called to *help* the ministry.

"For the same cause also do ye joy, and rejoice with me. But I trust in the Lord Jesus to send Timotheus shortly unto you, that I also may be of good comfort, when I know your state. For I have no man likeminded, who will naturally care for your state. For all seek their own, not the things which are Jesus Christ's.
- Philippians 2:18-21

Paul said, "It'll be good comfort to me to send Timothy, because I'll know what your state is. I'll know exactly what condition you're in because he and I are likeminded." *Likeminded* means "of the same mind and same understanding". When you choose people to be in the ministry, you're looking for those who naturally think like you do. They should not have to be forced to love people. "I don't know if I agree with the way Pastor's going to handle that. I'll do it because I know how to submit, but I don't like it and I don't agree with it."

"Why are you doing it that way?"

"Pastor wants it done that way."

They just threw the pastor under the bus. They also subtly expressed their disagreement. He said, "Timothy, by his nature, will care for you. It's not a hard thing for him; it's not difficult. He doesn't have to argue with himself to do so. He naturally desires the things that I desire." He said, "I don't have anyone else comparable to that. Nobody else thinks the way I think, does what I do. The rest of them, they're after their own."

Let's say the pastor leaves the church for the first time and he assigns you preach. However, you want to give a message that you wouldn't be teaching if he were in the room. So now he has to be concerned about whom he can put up on the pulpit in his absence. "I've been dying to tell them such-and-such! I'm going to get up there... Boy, I'm going to preach the paint off the walls!" You better sit down and wait until you're ready. They're seeking their own.

"I can't wait to get up there! Boy, I got the fire in me! I'm going to get up there, woo!"

Really? They're seeking their own.

Paul said, "I only have one guy, Timothy, who naturally thinks the same way I think. He moves how I move; he'll care about you the way I care about you. If I'm gone, Timothy will still do it the way I would because we are cut from the same cloth."

Similarly, this is also a problem with young men and women who are looking for a relationship. They're not choosing people that are cut from the same cloth, they're choosing people based on their visual observations. They're choosing the President based on the campaign, not on the history. They're out there shaking hands and kissing babies, putting their best foot forward and people fall for that. Next thing you know, they're wondering "Wait a minute, how did I get here?" They chose for reasons that are not based on who that person is, but rather what they want them to be.

Often, people will dismiss their rebellious behavior by saying that they just have their own opinions and preferences. The truth of the matter is nobody asked them for their opinion.

Opinions are earned with me. There are those whom I ask for their opinion, and they know who they are. Some will ask "Well how come Pastor doesn't ask me for my opinion?" The answer is pretty simple; I do not wish to have your opinion. Now, if you earn the right to speak into a situation, no problem. Still, you must *earn* it. How do you earn it? It comes when you consistently demonstrate your faithfulness. Leaders need to know you will naturally do what they would do, that you will care the way they care, that you understand the way that they understand.

Could you imagine if your pastor was frustrated and said, "I'm going to somebody else's church to preach. I don't like the way this crowd looks at me." That doesn't make any sense. I'm going to stick with what God gave me and I'm looking for those that are like Timothy — the ones who naturally will care for the state of the people. They don't have to work hard to do it, they don't have to change their whole DNA to be what God's asked them to be, it's just in them. They can't help but love; they can't help but care and serve because it's in their heart! Nothing is too much; nothing is above ordinary, and nothing is more than what they're willing to give. They just understand that it is what it is and God will never leave them nor forsake them. God will always return whatever they've done and so they're not keeping score.

They are not the ones who grab a mop as soon as the pastor enters the building just so he/she sees them mopping the floor. If that's what you do it for, you've got your reward. What are we doing this for, what is this all about? Why do we do this?

Why do *you* do it?

Paul said, "I have nobody else who will naturally care for your state and do this as I want it to be done." Why was that important? Paul had the ministry, he was the leader, and he was responsible. In

Galatians 2, we see just how concerned Paul was about his responsibilities.

> *I went in response to a revelation and, meeting privately with those esteemed as leaders, I presented to them the gospel that I preach among the Gentiles. I wanted to be sure I was not running and had not been running my race in vain.*
> *Gal 2:2 (NIV)*

Even though Paul was the leader, he still went to the elders and said, "This is what I've been preaching, what do you think? This is what I'm telling the gentiles, are you okay with this?" He still understood that even though he had the ministry, he had to be held accountable by the leaders in the ministry. How did he recognize that submission? He understood he couldn't do it all by himself.

There are people to whom I am personally submitted . I have spiritual parents that speak into my life and I share things with them because they're responsible for keeping me on track. In the same way, when Paul said, "Follow me as I follow Christ," that's your job. Follow your leader as they follow Christ.

If at any moment in time they are not following Christ, stop following, please. If they start following something like a head of lettuce, then you should say, "Look Pastor, I love you, but I have to go..."

However, if they're following God and preaching the Word of God, your job is to help. Your job is to bring your supply and learn. Your job is to not be too familiar, to recognize your position, and know you're in training and development mode. That's what this is really all about. If you're not training for ministry then you're supposed to be out there doing ministry. You only go through boot camp for a period of time. After that, you go to war. You are not in the church to occupy a seat. You are either learning how to do it, or you're going out and doing it. There is no betwixt.

THE ART OF PREPARATION

The unique challenge of training the body of Christ has been delegated to its leaders. All people are in different stages of development. Some are in baby stages; they cry about everything. Some are in their mature ages where they understand and they just do what is necessary to get the job done. Some are in a rebellious stage; they resemble teenagers; ten feet tall and bulletproof with all the answers. The leadership is still responsible for everyone.

I could turn my back on leadership and find a way to get over any offense they could have brought, but how do we turn our backs on Christ? How do people just walk away from Jesus? People fail to recognize that familiarity is the key reason why many are called, but few are chosen. It takes a unique group of individuals to acknowledge that if they're going to make it, they need to understand spiritual principles. As for the things they don't understand, they need to wait and judge it against the Word. It's bizarre how people judge their own lives in comparison to their surrounding environment. Every person that has flat out left the church I pastor has never come to me and said, "Pastor, I have a problem with this doctrine and here's why." Never. They measure themselves among themselves and the Bible says those people aren't wise. When you measure yourself against what you feel, your feelings will always validate themselves. "A house divided against itself shall not stand." (Mark 3) Your soul will validate what your soul thinks. So now all of a sudden, the plan of God for your life has been derailed. Some of you think you will figure it out later, but what if there is no "later"?

I don't know about you, but I don't want second best. I want God's absolute best. I want whatever it is that He has for me. The Bible says that you may prove (or "experience") what is the good, the acceptable and the perfect will of God (Romans 12). I don't want what is considered "good enough"; I don't even want what is considered acceptable unto God. I want the perfect will of God! In the perfect will of God comes massive success. In the perfect will of God comes the provision that God has for me! Not what's "good enough", not what's "acceptable", but what is perfect. To get there, you need to be cut from a different cloth.

The fifty-eight men that left must have thought they had to eat Jesus! What would you have done? Are you one of those twelve that said, "Yeah if I have to eat him, start the fire; let's get this party jumping"? How crazy and radical were they to stick around at a moment where Jesus told them they have to eat his flesh and drink his blood?

We have popcorn ministries where people pop up, and then they're gone. Firecrackers, flashes in the pan. They talk the game and then twenty years later say, "I remember the good old days. I remember back when..." as if God somehow fell off the throne. God didn't fall off the throne; they fell out of fellowship with Him. They lost their divine connection. God put you in divine relationships for a reason. Some of you don't see what that reason is. I'm sorry for you, but those that do see it will recognize and understand that God did it that way on purpose! It's designed to develop you, to knock off the edges. Every time you hear something that hits you the wrong way, you should be saying, "Yes! I just grew!" Not, "Is he ever going to preach a different message?" As soon as you change, I promise I'll write about something else. Until then, I'm a one-trick pony. I want you to be successful in the ministry. I want you to go on.

I'm not graded on my effort in that matter; I'm graded on the results. I'm not a fan of sports that say "Everybody wins!" No, not everybody won. Likewise, I don't condone creating competitiveness in your child to where they're unsportsmanlike either. As a former employer of people, we are dealing with a generation of people that were brought up to believe that you reward effort rather than results. Now, they come into the workplace and think they deserve a paycheck just for showing up. They're texting on their phone instead of working, but they showed up. In their minds, they really think, "You ought to be glad that I am here." How did we get there? Because we started this nonsense of, "Well Johnny at least you tried."

Listen, you praise effort. "Johnny, you did such a good job."

But you reward results.

People have mixed that up, and there are self-entitled children as a direct result of it. They've been rewarded for trying so now when the company says, "We need some results," their first answer is, "Well I tried." Nobody cares that you tried, not at this level. We want to know, "Can you do?" I am not graded on your efforts— I'm graded on the fruit and the success of your life. My report card is not graded on whether you showed up; my report card gets A's on it because you walk in what God has called you to be, and I played the part he asked me to in that process. If you're looking to sit and be comfortable, your leadership will be constantly hitting you and challenging you to move on and to move forward and to step up and to step out— We are not graded on your presence. We are graded on your fruit. It is the saddest day when you hire somebody that thinks their mere presence warrants their paycheck. They'll say, "I'm trying. Can't I get some credit for trying?" Sure. How about a pat on the back (which is about twelve inches above a kick in the butt)?

If you want a reward, your rewards come when you produce fruit. Your rewards come when you work not just talk. In James, Chapter 1, verses 23-24, the Bible tells us to not be a person who sees ourself in the mirror and then walks away and forgets who we are. It's not just about trying, it's about doing.

"Well, I know I'm called Pastor, I just wish God would tell me what he wants me to do."

"Hey, could you do me a favor? Could you sweep the floor?"

"I know I'm called, but I just wish God would tell me what to do."

"Hey, we need some help in this sound booth.Do you mind helping out back there?"

"Man, I know I'm called, I just sure wish God would tell me what to do!"

It's such a saddening state that we live in, but this is where we are as a society. It's so important to understand this is why many are called, and few are chosen. There are things God has for each and every one of you. The worst thing in the world is to watch people with no vision, because they perish.

Chapter Three:
The Art of Apprenticeship

"And he took the mantle of Elijah that fell from him, and smote the waters, and said, Where is the Lord God of Elijah? And when he also had smitten the waters, they parted hither and thither: and Elisha went over."
- 2 Kings 2:14

The first responsibility given to me while I was in training for ministry was to be a greeter. My second responsibility was to be an usher. After that, I became the Captain of the Ushers. Then, I launched a publication company for the church. As time went on, I continued to grow in my responsibilities. The training process comes through the local church. It is bizarre to me how many people seek after the plan of God for their lives, but yet they do not seek it within the church. They think somewhere along the line they will be placed into pulpit ministry because they feel a calling to teach. When asked if they feel called to teach, if they're assigned to kids ministry sometimes their response is, "Well I don't want to do that." Well then let's be honest, you're not called to teach. When I was developing in my church, I wanted to teach the kids, but my pastor wouldn't let me. He would tell me, "Look I need you in the sanctuary, so we just have to find other people to teach." I'd go in there, teach in a heartbeat and have a blast!" I'll do it now too. Honestly I'd rather teach some of them then some of these "adults". I love to see people learn. That's the hallmark of the teaching gift. You love to see people get it.

It amazes me how many people do not realize that, through the process of attending and serving in the church, your ministry is developed. Whether it takes 10-20 years— however long, it may be is up to you— the development occurs in the local church. That is why everyone should have a pastor. The responsibility of the pastor is to recognize the gifts that are in you and help you develop them, but it's strange how people think, "If I'm called to teach then somehow there's going to be a way that I'll just learn how to teach and I'll get up there and do it." They're looking for opportunity as opposed to education.

It is not easy to flow in the things of the spirit. I don't have timed messages that are written out point-by-point, *"3 Keys To A Better Life, Tomorrow!"* That is not my style of preaching. I used to wish it were, but it is not. Often when I'm teaching and preaching, I'm lead by inspiration. When everyone else is getting revelation, at times I'm getting it too. That's a different style.

Sometimes, people hear of the way we, at Stonepoint, operate, and they will say, "Well, why do we have to do all that? Why do we have to create an atmosphere? Why do we have to protect the anointing on your life?" We have to; otherwise I will be on the pulpit and have nothing to say. Often times, I don't have a message until I get on the platform or until I'm driving to the church. Do you know how frustrating that is?

Most people have their messages written a week in advance. They're studying and putting final touches on it. Me? I'm getting in the car just before service saying, "God, really? Help a brother out!" Yet and still when I arrive, He always shows up for me and that's by way of the anointing. It is getting easier for me to do that but in the natural

— as a person who is well planned— I think about plans and strategies all the time. It's very difficult (to me) for God to use me in a very spontaneous nature.

However, these are things concerning the holy spirit that I had to learn from someone who went through it. I could have affiliated myself with any other pastor, but some of them wouldn't understand. I had to find people that understood the ways of God so I could get answers. I mastered this through the instruction of my spiritual father. He said, "Son, the reason why you're struggling is because you don't preach as everybody else preaches. The difference is you're a Holy Ghost man and by flowing with the Holy Ghost, your understanding is different."

Occasionally, revelation comes out of my mouth and I'm hearing it for the first time. He's teaching me while He's teaching the congregation. These are things in and of the spirit.

If you are going to be associated with a spirit-filled church that is willing to allow the Holy Ghost to lead, then you must become skillful with the things of the spirit. We extend you an opportunity; we let you get involved in serving in the church. Why? To watch you, see how you handle pressure and aggravation. When someone ticks you off; we want to know how you handle it. Some of you just aren't ready yet. People believe that adversity builds character. That is a lie. Adversity does not build character, adversity reveals character.

We allow people to go through that process. You get involved over here and then you get promoted over there. It's amazing how you bring people up in the organization, yet if their minds are not renewed to what they are doing, they will bring substandard character, a lousy attitude, and the ways of the world all the way up into the high ranks of the group.

Now, everyone in the church struggles trying to get on the same page because you will not get there if you cannot discern spiritual things or your affect on the church. You cannot understand whether you're supposed to be here or not.

You have a supply. People need you, and they're looking to you. However, when you don't perceive the cog in the wheel that you are, and when you're failing to manage your responsibilities correctly, you affect other people. The Bible says that God set members in the body as He desired (1 Corinthians 12), but if the member does not stay where they're supposed to, it brings *"dis-ease"* to the body. As a result, we're looking for you to help in the kid's ministry, but if you do not show up, the whole organization has to shift at the last minute in order to cover your absence.

You're still growing and developing. It's amazing how many people think they have a call of God, but they don't feel impelled to participate in the organization, as if the call of God is going to come into your life and be developed outside of those doors. If it is, you are not supposed to be here. The local church is the place where your gift is developed.

It doesn't matter what your talents are per se because your talent is not always in line with your gift. That's the difference between natural and *super*natural understanding. People don't always perceive what their real gift is. Naturally, they think, "Well I'm skilled at smiling." You may be used as a greeter for awhile, but make no mistake about it. If we are doing the job correctly, we should be recognizing there's something more in you. So now what do you need to do? Build your character. Why do you need character? If you ever let your anointing out-develop your character, the anointing will open doors that your character won't let you stay in.

The reality is when you are not skilled at what you're doing; you lose proficiency. No one should have to beg you to get involved and plead, "We need your help!" You know you have a supply, you are called of God and you have a responsibility. Yet and still, when the pastor asks for some people to teach in the kid's area... "*...cricket... cricket...*"

I asked this question once to our congregation, "Who in here believes they're called to teach?" You should have seen the hands go flying up. Then I said, "Where's the kids teacher so we can sign these people up?" Hands dropped back down just as quickly as they went up. It was amazing!

If you have a gift, you better find somebody that will pull the gift out of you. That's the role and the responsibility of those that have been tasked with helping you grow. I've had people say, "Oh I just can't drive that far." I used to hear the voice of the Spirit telling me that I needed to get into more of my spiritual father's meetings. So there I was thinking, "Okay, well then I need some money because he travels all over this country and I don't have that kind of money. I'll catch him when he comes to Phoenix." Then the Lord said to me, "What are you doing to do about getting in those meetings?" I said, "I ain't going to do nothing about it until you send him over here!"And then the Lord never said another word about it.

When I did go to one of his meetings, I received an impartation. In my spirit, the Lord said to me, "You want to move fast, or you want to go slow? If you want to move at the clip that I'm trying to call you to, you need to get in his meetings." So you know what I did? I started looking at the calendar and I said, "Where is this man going to be? I'm at least going to go once a quarter."

I picked one, and decided that I was going. I did not know where the money would come from, but I was going. Every single time, the finances came to make those trips possible. Why? I discerned and understood my supply. I recognized that my obligation was to do ,as I was instructed, by God.

"Is it not to deal thy bread to the hungry, and that thou bring the poor that are cast out to thy house? When thou seest the naked, that thou cover him; and that thou hide not thyself from thine own flesh? Then shall thy light break forth as the morning, and thine health shall spring forth speedily: and thy righteousness shall go before thee; the glory of the Lord shall be thy reward."
--Isaiah 58:7-8

If you would serve and help people in the ministry, it will provide health and healing to your physical body and your bones. How do we not understand our responsibility to bring our supply? Now, my spiritual father will look at me and say, "You know, I appreciate you coming, you sure do help me." He's telling me that my presence pulls on the gift that's in him. I'm developed by the gift that's coming out of him. I recognize divine relationships and I understand where I'm supposed to be in the body. God has set members in the body as He has desired.

I would, and have driven 4-5 hours to be in his meeting, just to turn around and drive 4-5 hours to get back home. You would ask yourself, "Why would you have to do all that?"

"Night and day praying exceedingly that we might see your face, and might perfect that which is lacking in your faith?"
--1 Thessalonians 3:10

There's something about him seeing my face to help perfect what is lacking in my faith.

You are in the same situation. Your supply is necessary to the body— unless you're a spiritual vampire that just comes to suck the blood out of the body of Christ. You come to get what you can, and leave. I will warn you, be very careful and recognize that's a bad place to be.

Leadership helps people and trains them up through the ranks in the organization. They get close to the top, become offended, and work themselves right back down. They come off of staff; they get into the crowd, and next thing you know they disappear; all because of offense and not recognizing their supply.

You don't leave a church, you're sent from a church. Nowhere in the Bible do you hear anybody saying, "Well, I *was* going to that Corinthian Church, but I think I'm going over to Ephesus." If you know you're in the church you belong to, you don't leave it, you're sent from a church.

Now, how are you sent?

First, you are equipped, established, tried and tested. Then you are approved and you are sent to do the work that God has called you to do. You do it under the auspices of the organization that sent you. That way you go with the anointing, the covering and the protection that is afforded by the organization. A piece of it goes with you.

"Well, I'm an evangelist."

"Who's your pastor?"

"I don't have one."

"You're not an evangelist."

"I'm a prophet to the nations!"

"Who's your pastor?"

"I don't have one."

God didn't tell you that you need one? He's going to tell you everybody else's business, but He can't tell you what you're supposed to do?

I want you to be taught and trained correctly, because when I get to heaven I want God to say, "Whoo boy! These kids are sharp!" not, "Now I got a thousand dummies trying to figure out the plan for their life." Your plan is in the local church. "Well, I don't feel like I'm called to work with the kids." Nobody asked you that. Your ability to do what you don't want to do demonstrates your submission.

"God and Jesus and angels backed me up in these instructions. Carry them out without favoritism, without taking sides. Don't appoint people to church leadership positions too hastily. If a person is involved in some serious sins, you don't want to become an unwitting accomplice."
-- 1 Timothy 5:21-22 MSG

He said, "without favoritism, without taking sides." Some leaders will promote so-and-so only because they like them.

I don't care if I like you or not, I need to know your character. I don't promote people because I like them- although that certainly helps- but I need to know that they're faithful. I need to know they're obedient to the call and they'll do whatever it takes. They won't send me garbage or waste my time; they'll perform with excellence. I'm watching their behavior.

It's similar to Daniel 6:4 where the presidents and princes sought occasion against him, but that they couldn't find any. He was the type of person who operated with the spirit of excellence. Wait until you see that in a person as they go through adversity and challenges.

I love it when I keep telling people, "This is what I want you to do..." If I need to keep saying it, that tells me one of two things; either I'm a poor communicator, or they aren't listening. Yet, they all rally around the idea, "We want more people to come to Christ, we want to grow! We want to see expansion!" How is that possible when one person will have to do everything? It says don't put people in leadership too quickly. The King James translation says "Lay hands on no man suddenly". That doesn't mean, "Don't choke anyone quickly." To lay hands on no man suddenly means "don't commission them to ministry too quickly."

I had a friend who knew me for 8-9 years, and they'll still come to church every once in awhile, usually when their life falls apart. They come back; I help them put their life back together, and after they get where they think they should be, they leave. Then when their life falls apart again, they come back. I've been telling this person that if they want to get in ministry, they need to find somebody, submit themselves to them, and be developed by that man or woman of God. If they say, "Go sit in the corner," then go sit in the corner. If that person tells them. "This is what you're going to do from this point forward..." then go do it.

The last time I told him that, he left and went to a different meeting. In this meeting, a guy was standing on the platform preaching. The guy stops preaching and he says to this man, "You, come here. You're supposed to be in the ministry. What's your name?" He told him his name. The guys laid hands on him, and said, "I now commission you to go forward and flow in the office of an Evangelist. You are now separated into the ministry. Go and do it."

So shortly after, he calls me and he says, "I'm an Evangelist!"

I said, "According to whom?"

"Well, you see what happened was..."

"You got to be kidding me, do you know this guy?"

"No".

"Are you submitted to his ministry?"

"No."

"A guy you don't know, in a church you don't go to, who has never met you before, has commissioned you into an office and you don't see the problem with that?"

Eventually, a series of events happened in his life and he's still not operating in the things God has for him, but thinks he is. Satan is very deceptive. Just because you pick up in the spiritual realm that somebody's supposed to be an Evangelist doesn't mean that God gave you the authorization to commission them to do so. As this man was speaking and flowing, he's operating in the gifts and he recognized the call, but God didn't tell him to commission anyone yet. This guy spends his time in the club every Saturday, but now he's an Evangelist? Saving who- and from what?

This is how things unfold when you move outside of your supply. There's nothing more dangerous than to think that you are something you are not anointed to be. When you get out there and start dealing with devils and demons, they're going to look at you as they did to the Sons of Sceva. The Sons of Sceva were beaten, stripped naked and sent running. They were in a place where they should not have been trying to operate in an anointing they did not understand.

This is why God had enough sense to set you with people to make impartations into you and help you become skilled. Even if you say, "Well I don't think I'm called to the ministry." You still need to be skillful in the things of the spirit.

In Luke 13, the woman with the spirit of infirmity was bowed up for 18 years. How is it that the disciples and the Pharisee's couldn't heal her, but Jesus came along, told the Spirit of infirmity to loose her, and she straightened up? They did not understand spiritual things. They thought her back was broken, but when they tried to treat it, nothing changed. Jesus operated in the gift of discerning of spirits and recognized it was a spiritual issue. So here comes Jesus and upon seeing the woman with the bad back, he recognizes that it's a spirit of

48

infirmity harassing her. The spirit of infirmity itself was bowed up, and when it started to harass her body, she bowed up. When he cast the spirit out, she straightened up. Did she have a bad back? No. What she had was a spirit of infirmity attacking her and harassing her. That's what caused the symptoms of a bad back. This is an example of why development in the things of, and pertaining to, the spirit are crucial.

In Mark 9:25 when the little boy was deaf and dumb, Jesus said, "Thou deaf and dumb spirit leave him." When the spirit was rebuked, the boy both heard and spoke. How is it that the deaf and dumb spirit heard? The boy could not hear or speak. Jesus said to him, "Deaf and dumb spirit come out." The disciples were wondering how Jesus was able to get this boy healed. Jesus told the Disciples that it is but by prayer and fasting that this kind comes out.

Can the disciple's fasting help someone else? Can your own prayer and fasting do anything for somebody else? Why would Jesus say "It's by prayer and fasting that this spirit comes out?" Prayer and fasting puts you into a spiritual condition where your sensitivity to the realm of the spirit increases and you can discern spiritual things. They were thinking and responding carnally. They thought he didn't have ear-drums and couldn't speak due to him not having vocal cords. Jesus comes in, and by the spirit he discerned that it was a spiritual attack, and he dealt with it accordingly.

You may think, "Well I'm not called to the ministry, therefore, I don't need to be proficient." You better believe you do! There will be attacks on your body, in your life, and in your family that are definitely spiritual. You must learn how to be proficient in the things of the spirit so that when you see it, you'll know exactly what it is. You won't be trying to figure out, "Is it a bad back?" No, it's a spiritual thing. You need some spiritual proficiency whether you're in the ministry or not.

However, how much more, if you are in the ministry, do you need to be skilled to deal with these attacks?

I traveled everywhere with my pastor. He didn't preach a message in eight years that I didn't hear. I went wherever he went and I carried his Bible wherever he went. I carried his luggage into his hotel room wherever he went; I went at my own expense. I didn't ask, "Hey, can I bunk up with you?" Everybody asked, "Why are you following Pastor around? You must be his pet. Why are you carrying his stuff?" I was not stupid. I recognized that if I wanted to learn how to do something, I better find somebody who does and then learn from them. I can learn two ways as to what a T-bone steak looks like. One, I can ask the butcher— my preferred method. Two, I can stick my head up a cow's behind to find out. It's dark in there and well you get the point. I learned a long time ago that is not something I want to do.

I've always had a mentor, even in corporate business because I understood that I can learn from their experiences quickly and hopefully avoid their mistakes. Today, people complain, "Well, I don't want to submit. I don't like his personality." Listen, I don't care how my pastor spoke to me because I knew he was telling me the truth and he cared about me. That was all I needed. If he was frustrated and spoke out of his frustration, I was strong enough to handle that. I was grown enough to hear the message and not the messenger. I understood that the anointing is not taught, it is caught. Hiding in the side-lines will never allow the anointing to work into your life. The only way that happens is when you are working closely with a leader and you will see it rub off on you. It's the way it works.

This is what the local church is designed for. It's not just a place for you to assemble; it's a place for you to be trained. It's a place for you to be developed and where you can safely operate in spiritual things. If you miss it, the leadership is going to catch it.

"And it came to pass, when the Lord would take up Elijah into heaven by a whirlwind, that Elijah went with Elisha from Gilgal. And Elijah said unto Elisha, Tarry here, I pray thee; for the Lord hath sent me to Beth-el. And Elisha said unto him, As the Lord liveth, and as they soul liveth, I will not leave thee. So they went down to Beth-el. And the sons of the prophets that were at Beth-el came forth to Elisha, and said unto him, Knowest thou that the Lord will take away thy master from thy head to day? And he said, Yea, I know it; hold ye your peace."
-- 2 Kings 2:1-3

Now, these are sons of prophets which means— for all intensive purposes in this book— we can call them baby prophets. They picked up in the realm of the Spirit what was about to happen. Here is a great example of how this works: We will ask somebody to come up to the pulpit and read some announcements. We give them a pre-written script, but because they start to discern my message, they start to talk about my message. They're picking up what is about to happen, but they're not the ones who were told to say it; I am. As my spiritual grandmother, Pastor Nancy Dufresne, would say, "What they're supposed to do is pick the gun up, put the bullets in and put it back down so that when I get there, I fire the gun based on holding the highest office in this church." People don't always understand spiritual things so they will pick up what's about to happen and take it as a sign to run with it. I can't tell you how many times I've had people come up and say things about the message that were wrong, or they stood up after the message and brought light to a part of it that was not the main idea. See, when I ended the message, I left the congregation where I wanted them. I call it "book-ending" the message. They start framing it out in a different way and they've lost proficiency in the spirit. They did not recognize that they were out of pocket.

I was in one of my spiritual father's meetings. While he's sitting down and had not yet got up to preach, the pastor of that church stood up and called a healing line. Now they brought my spiritual father in to minister healing; so he's sitting and waiting. The pastor starts talking about healing when they were supposed to be receiving an offering. He picked up what was happening in the spirit, but he was supposed to load the gun and put it down. Proficiency in the realm of the spirit is absolutely critical. While of course we can all minister healing, however, it certainly would have been better to yield to the highest anointing in the room to get the best results.

Dr. Ed Dufresne had a very strong healing ministry. Accounts have been given that when he went into a particular church, a couple weeks before he arrived, his anointing would start to roll in. People would be healed before he even showed up.

A lack of skill and proficiency in the spirit is why at times you will see people that pull others aside privately in the parking lot and give them a prophecy. We had a young man at our church that thought he was a prophet swore he was and knew he was one. He called me and said he wanted me to be his spiritual father. I took him to a restaurant and tried everything I could do to talk him out of his request for spiritual fatherhood. He would pull people aside to give them prophesies in the lobby and out in the parking lot. So I took him aside, explained why that was inappropriate and showed it to him in scriptures. Prophesy is edification, exhortation and comfort. Every one of us can prophesy, but not every one of us is a prophet. If it comes with revelation, then you are moving out of general prophecy and you are moving into the revelation gifts of the spirit. Now, if you are doing that, the Bible says: "Let the prophets speak two or three, and let the other judge."
-- 1 Corinthians 14:29

People think they're prophesying but really they're prophe-*lying*. Prophesy is just general exhortation. You don't pull people in the church aside and say, "Well the Lord told me to tell you..." Okay, so let me see if I understand this correctly. The Lord skipped over all the

52

recognized and sanctioned leadership in the church and told you to deliver a message? It doesn't work that way. If you are out in the street and God tells you to go say something to a person, as long as it is God, go ahead.

Here's the thing; the sons of the prophets knew that Elijah was going to be leaving Elisha. What if (in the realm of the spirit) there was something you heard that I heard too- but God told me not to say it yet? Then you, with your happy and zealous self, go and tell somebody something and it was not the time for them to hear it? You have just caused spiritual damage in the body.

You have to learn these things. I learned it while sitting across the table from my pastor at Starbucks. I didn't learn everything from the pulpit; I got it in my relationship with him playing video games at times. If he was talking a lot, I try to keep the game going as long as I could just so I could get more information. I understood my relationship; it was divine. I knew that I was there to get something from him and I recognize that I had to do whatever it took to be in the right relationship with him. I never spoke unless he spoke to me. Other people would be around him and his reaction to their presence would be *Ugh!* He would be with me, and I didn't have anything to say until I was spoken to. I didn't take it personally. We've driven 3-4 hours in the car and never said more than a few words and I was good with it. I understood his personality and I recognized it was my job to build that relationship with him, to make him comfortable so that he'll begin to share these things with me. I didn't think that he would just have to put up with me talking a lot. If I thought that way, then he probably wouldn't want to be around me. He wouldn't ask me to join him every time he went somewhere, but I was available. Sometimes I'd sit out in front of his office in a chair. I'd sit there at a little table and work on the computer.

He'd ask me, "What are you doing?"

"Just hanging out." Being available.

He'd walk out of his office, see me and say, "Hey, I was thinking about getting some coffee..."

I would immediately chime in, "What do you want, Starbucks? What kind? I'll go run and bring it back." Next thing you know, when I demonstrated proficiency of my service, he then asked me to do other things. He's inviting me to meetings and to go do things with him.

No one has been taught today how to flow in the things of God. It's tragic because people are being robbed by Satan every single day. People have come to the church I pastor and I've heard them make remarks such as, "Oh yeah I've been getting blessed, I've been prospering." Then they leave unexpectedly and without notice.
"I can get that from anywhere." No, you can't. If you could have, you already would have. There's obviously something about the church and the anointing upon it that is blessing your life. I'm like Paul; he said he wasn't afraid to magnify his office. Me personally, I'm absolutely nothing, but I will refuse to let the office in which I stand be diminished. Your church is the one that will feed your spirit, supply you and bring you to a place where you can be used of God. I'm convinced of it; I'm sure of it. The baby prophets picked up Elisha's situation correctly, but he told them to hold their peace, stop being so zealous and just be quiet.

"And Elijah said unto him, Tarry, I pray thee, here; for the Lord hath sent me to Jordan. And he said, As the Lord liveth, and as thy soul liveth, I will not leave thee. And they two went on."
-- 2 Kings 2:6

Notice, Elijah kept trying to get rid of Elisha. He constantly responds to Elijah that he is not leaving. He was staying with the one that God had connected him with because he recognized his supply.

"And Elijah took his mantle, and wrapped it together, and they were divided hither and thither, so that they two went over on dry ground. And it came to pass, when they were gone over, that Elijah said unto Elisha, Ask what I shall do for thee, before I be taken away from thee. And Elisha said, I pray thee, let a double portion of thy spirit be upon me."
-- 2 Kings 2:8-9

How did Elisha get the double portion? He was faithful. Elijah said, "If you're with me, if you'll stay, it will happen." He did not say, "If you leave early..." Or, "If you come out from under..." Or "If you get offended and leave..." He said, "If you stay with it, the double portion will come upon you."

Kenneth Hagin Sr. used to say that he wanted his ceiling to be our floor. Everyone would think, "This man has a huge multi -acre campus, a successful ministry, a sanctuary that seats thousands... and he wants *his* ceiling to be *our* floor?" He understood if you stay with it, you'll get a double portion. If you stay with it, God will bless you double for your commitment. That's the way that it works. Listen, if I had another way to do it I promise you I would have done it.

"And he said, Thou hast asked a hard thing: nevertheless, if thou see me when I am taken from thee, it shall be so unto thee; but if not, it shall not be so."
-- 2 Kings 2:10

Now you think Elisha could have said to himself, "Hey wait a minute. I served this man for 20 years! Just because I chose to leave a minute early, all of my 20 years are now taken from me?" The race goes to those who finish, not those who start.

Some people in this generation think all they have to do is start. You don't need to start; you need to *finish*. That's what winners are all about. God needs people who are going to finish the race; that's why commitment is so indispensable. "I'm going to stay until it's done. I'm going to do what it takes to accomplish the goal." Many people start well, boy they come in with as much energy as a firecracker! They're on fire for God; they just want to serve! ...Until leadership asks, "Can I get you to help me with the kids?" Then, the answer is "Yeah, uh..." It's the way it works. All of a sudden the pastor says something you don't like, and your out the door on to the next ministry.

Let's continue the story about the young gentleman that I mentioned earlier in this chapter. I brought him to Starbucks. I had to chase him down for two days to get to him because he knew he messed up. I laid out scripture and I showed him the word of God, but I didn't see him for two weeks after that. He attended a few more services and then I never saw him again, and I'm his "spiritual father". I have people who acknowledge me as their spiritual father and they're still around. Why? I'm committed to them, which places me in that office in their life. But it's amazing how people can ask leaders to commit to them in a way that they are not willing themselves to return..

They easily come to me when they're not feeling well, or their lives are under attack. I'm the first one to come and pray with them, lay hands on them and believe God with them. When they get upset with me, they send an e-mail with their departure notice. It's absolutely cowardly and lacks integrity. Welcome to ministry. I guarantee if you need me and you're one of my spiritual children I'm there. When I come, help comes with me. I don't show up to worry or cry with you. We can cry a little bit, but after we get passed that, help shows up. I wouldn't send you an e-mail, "Wish you the best, but God's moving me on." See, it sounds insane doesn't it?

"And it came to pass, as they still went on, and talked, that, behold, there appeared a chariot of fire, and horses of fire, and parted them asunder; and Elijah went up by a whirlwind into heaven. And Elisha saw it, and he cried, My father, my father, the chariot of Israel, and the horsemen thereof. And he saw him no

more: and he took hold of his own clothes, and rent them in two pieces. He took up also the mantle of Elijah that fell from him, and went back, and stood by the bank of the Jordan' And he took the mantle of Elijah that fell from him, and smote the waters, and said, Where is the Lord God of Elijah? And when he also had smitten the waters, they parted hither and thither: and Elisha went over. "
-- 2 Kings 2:11-14

Didn't he just see Elijah do that? He imitated what he learned and it produced the same result.

"And when the sons of the prophets which were to view at Jericho saw him, they said, The spirit of Elijah doth rest in Elisha. And they came to meet him, and bowed themselves before him. And they said unto him, Behold now, there be with thy servants fifty strong men; let them go, we pray thee, and seek thy master: lest peradventure the Spirit of the Lord hath taken him up, and cast him upon some mountain, or into some valley. And he said, Ye shall not send. "
-- 2 Kings 2:15-16

When the sons of the prophets saw Elisha, they recognized that the spirit of Elijah was on him. Now they see the anointing on him and they're trying to tell him what he already knew. They were approaching Elisha as if they were on the same level as he was. The sons of the prophets said, "Let's send these men out to look for Elijah just in case God threw him on a mountain." Elisha said, "No, I know exactly where he is." However, since they insisted, he let them do it-which goes to show that you can't stop people from doing what they want to do. They acknowledge that the spirit of Elijah was upon him, yet they were not honoring him as they would have Elijah. They recognized the anointing on him, but they were not of the same level as he was. Yet and still they insisted on going, so he let them.

There are phases and rooms in the realm of the spirit, or "degrees" if you will. My spiritual father wrote a book called "*Phases and Rooms*". I would not submit myself to someone with a lower anointing than myself. Reverend Ricky Edwards is my Spiritual Father and Dr. Dufresne is my Spiritual Grand-Father. These are people that I turn to when I cannot get where I need to be on my own. That's also why you have a pastor and spiritual leaders- so when things are not where you want them to be in your life, there's an anointing on them for you. That's why we are called a gift to the body. The anointing on your leaders and upon your church is meant to help you deal with things that, at times, you may not be able to overcome. We all are part of the body and have a supply.

And the next day we that were of Paul's company departed, and came unto Caesarea: and we entered into the house of Philip the evangelist, which was one of the seven; and abode with him. And the same man had four daughters, virgins, which did prophesy. And as we tarried there many days, there came down from Judaea a certain prophet, named Agabus. And when he was come unto us, he took Paul's girdle, and bound his own hands and feet, and said, "Thus saith the Holy Ghost, So shall the Jews at Jerusalem bind the man that owneth this girdle, and shall deliver him into the hands of the Gentiles."
-- *Acts 21:8-11*

Philip had four daughters that could prophesy. They were not prophets, because it took a prophet named Agabus to reveal what was going to happen to Paul in Jerusalem. If they were prophets, why didn't they tell Paul? They had every opportunity to; he was staying with them, but they were not prophets. Just because a person can prophesy does not mean they have been promoted into the office of a prophet. Just because a person can preach and exhort, does not mean they are in the office of a pastor. There are gifts that God has given to people (like the gift of exhortation and the gift of evangelism). Some people will think, "Well I can lead others to the Lord, so I'm an Evangelist." That does not mean that you're an evangelist. If you are flowing in miracles and powerful signs that bring people to Christ, you *might* be an evangelist.

Many churches have been started by people who are not gifted to pastor, but they are gifted to preach. Some people are out prophesying to the world, but they are not prophets. If you are under the age of forty-five, you most likely are not a prophet; myself included. You don't have enough experience. You know how to prophesy and in some cases propheLIE. If that is what you're called to be, you will need some time to let that prove itself. The daughters of Philip could prophesy, yet they were not prophets.

You have to be very careful when you're trying to get into the ministry. It's not just about having the ability to get up and preach a message. You need a deep understanding of spiritual things to be able to discern them correctly. This same gentleman I mentioned earlier pulled somebody aside and gave them a prophesy. I knew in my spirit that he did it and I knew what he said. I pulled him over to me and I said, "Let me correct what just happened."
He asked, "Well how did you know what happened?"

I knew it by the spirit. God tells me what's going on with my sheep. There's a proficiency that is needed in the things of the spirit because anything you don't use correctly, you'll lose skill in. If you learn how to do something the wrong way, you'll do it under the pretense that it's correct when it's not.. Practice doesn't make perfect; perfect practice makes perfect. Then when you're not achieving good results, it becomes harder to do. I remember I was talking to a man who coaches kid's basketball and he said, "I prefer to work with the ones that have no experience. I can teach them how to play the right way without breaking down bad habits first."

How many times have people come into the church with bad habits? They're unskilled, not submissive and then wonder what the plan of God for their life is. "Nothing" is the plan of God for your life until you learn how to submit and do what you're asked to do with excellence- whether you like it or not.

If you ask me to do something and I tell you I'm going to do it, when you see it your reaction will be, "Wow! Now that's how something's supposed to be done." You won't know whether I liked it or not because I'll do it with the best that I have. That's the type of spirit that God honors and regards because he expects you, as a minister, to recognize your skill sets and where you drop off and where He begins. If you have no proficiency in the spirit, you'll struggle.

There are people that should be in the ministry, but they're not. They're hard-headed, stubborn and want to do things their way. Some of you should be so much further along right now that it's ridiculous. We have a responsibility to understand spiritual things. You have to know that just like those daughters who did prophesy, there are times in your life the gifts will come on you. You'll give a word of wisdom, but that doesn't mean you're a prophet, an evangelist, a teacher or a pastor. You may flow in different gifts at different times; that's the way God works in the body. If you don't understand that, then you'll get a big head. Then you start to think, "Pastor so-and-so doesn't recognize my gift. I'm going to go somewhere else that will use me and my gift."

You have an opportunity of a lifetime to be with a group of believers that will take the time to teach you spiritual things and help you develop and grow in the things of God. Do not miss it by remaining tough or hard-headed. All you have to do is make the adjustments. My pastor would preach messages that hit me in the head, but I wasn't mad for long. If I spit it out because I did not like it, then I wrote it down. I'd chew it until I could eat it.

The body of Christ is responsible for the things that it doesn't know and the things it does know. It's dangerous for you to come up to light and then walk away. People assume, "I'll just pick up where I left off." No, you will not. If you get out of line at a theme park, you go to the back of the line. You're going to start over from the beginning.

I can't tell you how many times people will say, "Pastor; I want to help do this and that..." And then they are nowhere to be found. There's nothing they can do if they're not present. The ministry runs every week; they have to be there.

"Well, I got this great idea!"

Nobody asked you for your ideas. Learn the way they do it first, then if you have suggestions, beautiful.

I have a table of Leadership Members and they're my suggestion box. If you want to put your suggestions in, then you must earn your place at the table. Until then, you don't have an opinion. It is always the one with the greatest criticism that does the least.

I want you to be skilled, proficient and walk out the plan that God has for you. I will continue to preach until people understand it. Once they "get it", there's no stopping them. If you do not understand spiritual things, you will be running in circles until you "get it". God does not honor your complaining, your crying, objections, or reasoning, but he will honor your faith.

When you have faith, the end result of that is faithfulness. We can count on you and depend on you. You are where you say you will be at the time you said you will be there; 11 o'clock, not a single minute (or five minutes) after. If you're early you're on time, if you're on time you're late, and if you're late that's unacceptable.

Chapter Four:
The Art of Relationship

"And some days after Paul said unto Barnabas, Let us go again and visit our brethren in every city where we have preached the word of the Lord, and see how they do. And Barnabas determined to take with them John, whose surname was Mark. But Paul thought not good to take him with them, who departed from them from Pamphylia, and went not with them to the work. And the contention was so sharp between them, that they departed asunder one from the other: and so Barnabas took Mark, and sailed unto Cyprus; And Paul chose Silas, and departed, being recommended by the brethren unto the grace of God. And he went through Syria and Cilicia, confirming the churches."
- Acts 15:35-41 KJV

Barnabas was in the ministry longer than Paul was. He was the one who gave him access to God's people. When Paul was known as Saul of Tarsus, he had a vile reputation for killing Christians, stoning them and beheading them.. His reputation caused the people not to trust him, so God joined Barnabas with Paul in order to bring him into the ministry.

Sometimes you deal with people that are older, that have been in the church or even in the ministry longer than you, but they do not have the level of revelation that you do. The Bible tells us to know no man after the flesh; we are to know them by the spirit (2 Corinthians 5). It says to know them that labor among you. The word *know* means "to see or perceive them correctly". In other words, recognize what part they play in your life.

When you talk to people about your position in their life, it can sound very self-glorifying. If you see me as "Gene", you'll miss it. However, if you recognize the office and the anointing that's in me then it will be clear what I can bring to your table. When you understand that, then you know when I show up, I come to help.

When you have a little pizza/paint party, there are always those that show up for the pizza but not the paint. When they arrived, help didn't come with them. They're looking for the food and the drinks; they want to know what's on TV; they didn't come to help. They did not perceive that they were invited to bring their supply. It was to ease the burden or ease the load. We all have the one friend who shows up with that bad kid in tow. They're there to help, but the one kid is tearing up everything else. You're like, "You know what, really? I got this. I'm good." They really brought pain and not assistance.

Now we can relate that to the situation between Barnabas and Paul. Barnabas was chosen to help Paul, but he felt that his opinion was greater than Paul's. He did not think that the ministry entrusted to Paul and not him. He was the one that should have come along to help.

It's like Moses holding up the rod. It was Moses' hand and rod that mattered. Even if Aaron had done jumping jacks, nothing would have happened. The more knowledgable people think they are, they become less concerned about the things of the spirit.

Now, here are Barnabas and Paul. Paul says, "I'm not taking John Mark because he ditched us" We read later on, Paul said, "Bring me John Mark for he is profitable." Paul was not punishing John Mark; he just knew his time had not come. A professed leader will not give someone more than they can take."Well, why was Paul so critical? How come Paul can't forgive? How come Paul can't let that go? Maybe John Mark did mess up..." He did. Paul did let it go, but Paul also knew better than to allow John Mark to hurt himself. John Mark did not know he was not ready. It's obvious he didn't know because he hooked up with Barnabas and left.

Let me ask you a question; Which book of the Bible did Barnabas write? Which one did John Mark write? They didn't write any of them. They went off together without spiritual discernment. They did not recognize the anointing upon Paul's life.

It's similar to the occurrence between Lot and Abraham in Genesis 13. Abraham said, "Listen, if you want to split up, you can take all that over there, and I'll take this over here.Or, we can switch it, I don't care." Lot and his people were getting into fights with Abraham's people. Abraham said, "We cannot have contention. You can take this side or that side; I don't care, pick one. You can take the best of it or the worst of it. However, I know one thing is certain; if you give me the worst, God will turn it around for my good. If you give me the bottom, God will make it the top. I understand that the anointing is on me."

Let's look back to Paul's situation. He decided to take Silas in Barnabas' absence. The people recognized Silas as the one who should go alongside Paul. He came into agreement with that and took Silas. However, notice the people did not pursue after Barnabas.

This is what happens when you sense ministry in your life, and you don't recognize that God assigned people to you that will help direct and cultivate that ministry. If you see your ministry as independent, you will not acknowledge or accept this fact.

This is the last time in scripture that you hear about Barnabas. He walked right off the pages of scripture. Evidently, John Mark put his life back into order because later Paul said, "Bring me John Mark, for he is profitable unto the ministry." Paul and Silas were in a dungeon together. Some theologians believe that they were waist-high in feces. What if Paul were in there with Barnabas? He needed to be with somebody who was not discerning the flesh, but the spirit. When all hell broke loose, he needed somebody that understood the power of God so they could worship together. When they worshiped God, the jail doors broke open, but it took Paul and Silas, not Paul and Barnabas, or Paul and John. If John Mark ran before, what do you think John Mark would do if he were neck-deep in trouble?

The flesh is what tells you to walk away from the ministry where God has planted you. There was sharp contention between them, so Barnabas unhooked. Leaving a church is only done under one premise; they're not teaching the Word anymore. Until then, leaving is a decision of the flesh. "Well, I just can't hook up with it." You better be careful because Barnabas walked right off the pages of the Bible. You do not hear any more stories about Barnabas' exploits, but you hear John Mark's name.

"Alexander the coppersmith did me much evil: the Lord reward him according to his works: Of whom be thou ware also; for he hath greatly withstood our words. At my first answer no man stood with me, but all men forsook me: I pray God that it may not be laid to their charge. Notwithstanding the Lord stood with me, and strengthened me; that by me the preaching might be fully known, and that all the Gentiles might hear: and I was delivered out of the mouth of the lion."
- 2 Timothy 4:14-17

My book, *"Identity: Discovering Your Authority In Christ"* was assigned to be edited by somebody who attended our church, but they abandoned that project. I know what it was; it was spiritual. Satan did not want that book to be published.. However, do you know how much damage a poorly made decision like that causes? You just leave, and the ministry is hanging out there in the balance. It just brought harm to the body. That's why the Bible says, "For many are sick, weak and some die" (1 Corinthians 11). They're not discerning the body or their part in it. You don't leave ministries unattended, or projects undone; its disrespectful. If you leave a job, you give them two weeks' notice. You do not approach your boss one day and say, "Hey, I'm out. Peace." You didn't get hired that way.

Some people don't leave well and that's why they're never invited back. Just about every job that I've ever left- with the exception of my first job at McDonalds- I can call and get a job because I left well. I didn't leave them in a lurch. Alexander the coppersmith did great harm to Paul, but he said, "The Lord will repay him." People are not afraid of damaging the body of Christ anymore. They just claim God has moved them on to something else. So He moved you on and left us in a lurch? You want to tell me you serve the same God I serve, but He doesn't love me as much as He loves you?

Paul told them to beware of Alexander because he greatly withstood the Word. Paul goes on to say, "At my first answer, no man stood with me but all men forsook me. I pray that it not be laid to their charge." In the first statement he's saying, "God's going to repay Alexander the coppersmith, but the other men left me out of fear for persecution, not because they wanted to bring harm." Paul becomes an indictor of the one who brought damage and an intercessor for those who were struggling.

If you want to be in ministry, you have to recognize the impact that you have. When you're assigned to do something, it should be done with excellence. When work is done poorly, you're agitating the rest of the body.

I made a point to not to be on my pastor's problem list. He had a problem list, just like every leader has one, but my goal was never to be on that list. If he asked me for a report, it was thorough. I answered all of his questions. He did not have to stress over the work I gave to him. I understood and I brought a supply to my man of God. As long as he was at peace with me, then the flow of the anointing from him would benefit my life. If you receive a righteous man in the name of a righteous man, you get a righteous man's reward.

Likewise, he who receives a husband in the office of a husband will receive the reward of a husband. The manner in which you acknowledge someone will allow or disallow you access to their gifts. Abraham violated God's instruction and brought Lot with him, and God still blessed him. Although there was strife between them, the anointing was on Abraham. If I was Lot and Abraham said, "Hey, do you know your people are causing problems?" My response would be to fire the offender and let Abraham know that I was truly sorry. He had a supply. You have a supply and need to learn how to recognize it.

The anointing on my spiritual father's life breaks yokes in the ministry entrusted to me. When you understand what supply is, then you'll understand authority.

Barnabas wanted to bring John Mark along, but Paul objected, so they left and Barnabas was never to be seen again. A powerful ministry; they were a good team. The Bible says that the Holy Ghost instructed, "Separate me Paul and Barnabas for the work I have called them to." They had a ministry together. Can you imagine Barnabas thinking, "Well I'm older than Paul in the ministry, and he should listen to me." Paul wrote three quarters of the New Testament, not Barnabas. It's always the people that begin to reject your leadership who produce the least amount of fruit. A leader's responsibility is not to hinder your ministry, but to keep your character under control.

"So Naaman came with his horses and with his chariot, and stood at the door of the house of Elisha. And Elisha sent a messenger unto him, saying, Go and wash in Jordan seven times, and thy flesh shall come again to thee, and thou shalt be clean. But Naaman was wroth, and went away and said, Behold I thought, He will surely come out to me, and stand, and call on the name of the Lord his God, and strike his hand over the place, and recover the leper. Are not Abana and Pharpar, rivers of Damascus, better than all the waters of Israel? May I not wash in them, and be clean? So he turned and went away in a rage."
- 2 Kings 5:9-12

The Word of the Lord came to Elisha, who gave it to Gehazi, (his servant). Gehazi delivered the message to Naaman, and the first thing Naaman said was, "Can I not go to another river?"
No, he couldn't go to another river.

When God gives instruction or does anything, He is very specific. Likewise, God has placed people in the body (in the church) where He desires. "I can just go to another church and get the same blessings." Not if God placed you somewhere else. I used to see people's health restored to them at my pastor's church. Shortly after that, they left, offended by the Word. Why would anyone walk away from their supply? See, if you were in a church where you were never blessed or taught anything, then I could understand considering another place. But to come to a place where the anointing is increasing your finances, your family and you're healed and blessed by it, how do you have the nerve, like Naaman, to say, "Can I go to the other river?" No!

"And his servants came near, and spake unto him, and said, My father, if the prophet had bid thee do some great thing, wouldest thou not have done it? How much rather then, when he saith to thee,

Wash, and be clean?"
- 2 Kings 5:13

In other words, "If he'd have asked you to do something complicated you'd have done it. This is simple."

"Then he went down, and dipped himself seven times in Jordan, according to the saying of the man of God: and his flesh came again like unto the flesh of a little child, and he was clean... But he said, As the Lord liveth, before whom I stand, I will receive none. And he urged him to take it; but he refused. And Naaman said, Shall there not then, I pray thee, be given to thy servant two mules' burden of earth? For thy servant will henceforth offer neither burnt offering nor sacrifice unto other gods, but unto the Lord. In this thing the Lord pardon thy servant, that when my master goeth into the house of Rimmon to worship there, and he leaneth on my hand, and I bow myself in the house of Rimmon: when I bow down myself in the house of Rimmon, the Lord pardon thy servant in this thing. And he said unto him, Go in peace. So he departed from him a little way. "But Gehazi, the servant of Elisha the man of God, said, Behold, my master hath spared Naaman this Syrian, in not receiving at his hands that which he brought: but as the Lord liveth, I will run after him, and take somewhat of him."
- 2 Kings 5:14-20

Now Elisha was not going to take Naaman's gifts. Why? Initially, Naaman was angry. He didn't believe, didn't submit; he still got his miracle, but Elisha said, "Now you want to come back and bless me?" That is the antithesis of faith. He was expecting Naaman to first believe, then receive. If Naaman had said, "Let me go ahead and bless you now, and then I'm going to the river," Elisha would have received it but Naaman obliviously brought it after he received what he asked for. What Elisha was looking for was a revelational experience, not a transactional one. So Gehazi went to receive the offering that Elisha rejected.

> *"But he went in, and stood before his master. And Elisha said unto him, Whence comest thou, Gehazi? And he said, Thy servant went no whither. And he said unto him, Went not mine heart with thee, when the man turned again from his chariot to meet thee? Is it a time to receive money, and to receive garments, and oliveyards, and vineyards, and sheep, and oxen, and menservants, and womanservants? The leprosy therefore of Naaman shall cleave unto thee, and unto thy seed forever. And he went out from his presence as a leper as white as snow."*
> *-- 2 Kings 5:25-27*

Elijah was taken away by chariots of fire, and he dropped his mantle upon Elisha. Elisha received a double portion and executed twice as many recorded miracles as Elijah did - the last of which was when he was dead. He is the only one recorded in the Bible, who performed a miracle while deceased. Elisha faithfully served Elijah. If Gehazi chose to serve Elisha faithfully, could you imagine the anointing he would have received? He did not achieve that due to his immoral character.

Here's what happens; he's operating on a borrowed anointing. Elisha told him, "Go tell Naaman to dip himself in the Jordan." Gehazi did as he was told. The anointing was with him because the man of God gave him the word; he was merely the carrier. Naaman is healed and Gehazi seemed to think that if people would do what he said, then they will be blessed! In his mind, the miracle was as much his doing as it was Elisha's. If Elisha didn't want the money, then Gehazi concluded that he would take it. Gehazi should have been in a position to walk in a quadruple anointing. I understand the concept of addition, but I love multiplication more. I can add something to your account, or I can multiply it. If Elisha inherited double what Elijah had, then if Gehazi remained faithful, submitted and supportive, he would have walked in an exceptionally powerful anointing. But when you hear the word "submission", most people equate that to "abuse". To be submitted does not mean you're abused.

Gehazi should have walked in double of what Elisha had, but his character took him off-course. He could not be trusted and was not faithful. When Elisha told Naaman "No," he meant just that. He was teaching a lesson, helping Naaman to know that the gift of God could not be bought. It's one thing to bring an offering out of honor, but it's another to try and purchase God's blessings. Some people who give think the pastor is going to do whatever they say. Honestly, most pastors don't care if you give 90% of the church's income. If you leave, God will bring someone else. The leaders don't serve you; they serve God. It can be utilized as a point of manipulation. Elisha recognized this and was making certain to not let Naaman think he can buy the anointing.

Now, Gehazi returns from collecting an unsanctioned offering, and Elisha says, "Where'd you go?" He gave him an opportunity to explain and repent. What did Gehazi do? "I didn't go anywhere, I was out back washing the Camel. Why did he lie?" Elisha said, "Did not my spirit go with you? Did not my heart go with you?" We understand the heart to be the spirit. He said, "Didn't my spirit go with you?" Then, he began to describe what he saw. "The Lord showed me. You ran up to them, and he gave you gifts. I saw it happen in the realm of the spirit. When you went, I went with you." If Elisha's spirit went with Gehazi when he was doing something wrong, then how much more do you think Elisha's spirit went with him if Gehazi might have been in trouble?

There's an anointing that assists people to deal with situations in their life because of their mere affiliation to the church. Had they not been a part of the organization, they would not have benefited from

72

it. How many times do you think Gehazi was protected from a problem because of Elisha's anointing?

When a company or business hires new people, they supply them equipment, right? Sometimes they need a computer, a truck, a car, or some tools. Whatever it is that you need, when you're hired you're given what you need. When God brings somebody into the ministry, he will equip them for the office in which they stand.

The President of the United States is absolutely nothing without his title. If he were not President, he would not have Air Force One or the Secret Service. He would not be flying all over the world or be the most powerful man in the world. It's his office that gives him the ability that he has! Whoever stands in that office will have what he has. He doesn't have a lifetime lease on the White House.
Paul said, "I magnify my office."

People want to get into ministry, but they do not understand that if you cannot follow the man you can see, you cannot follow the God you cannot see. When people disagree with you, that does not mean they seek to hurt you. Sometimes I have to disagree because I'm trying to protect you. Paul didn't want John Mark out in the battlefield at that time.. He still required some growth. Paul said he was not ready, but Barnabas decided that he was and took him for a ride along. The fact that he went was proof that he wasn't ready.

I came from an industry where apprenticing was not uncommon. If you don't think you need to be apprenticed, you are wrong. If you think God will pass you because of how old you are, you are wrong. You'll be the oldest first grader; will not even be able to fit in the little desk. You'll be sitting down amongst the kids with a beard and a mustache. Keep waiting, because you're discerning things after the flesh. God does not move in the flesh; He moves after the spirit. If you want to understand the things of the spirit, you better "get in where you fit in", recognize the supply that you have to bring, and let yourself be trained.

It's humorous to watch when the boss walks in the room and everybody straightens up to move into position. The one that does it when nobody's looking is the one God promotes. It's the one that's on it because it needs to be done; the one that recognizes there's a supply that has to be brought and they need to do it. Not doing it sloppily, lazily, half-heartedly and think God will bless that; because He will not.

God is no respecter of persons, but he is a respecter of faith levels. It's the higher faith level that says, "I'm bringing my supply. I'm going to make sure that if Pastor has a list of problems I will not be on it." It takes faith to be in that position and understand your supply. The ones who do not recognize are the ones who struggle with more problems. They tend to be the ones who have sickness in their body because they do not recognize that they're violating the rules. Barnabas should have said, "Oh you don't want to take John Mark? Okay, me neither. I don't even know what I was thinking. Whom do you want to take? Just take me. We can add anybody you want but could you please take me?" That would have worked, but, he saw Paul as an equal. When the pastor says, "We're going to reach out into the community and we're going to pray for people," the pastor is commissioning you to do a work. You go out there and all of a sudden you think, "Hey, I like ministering to people! I really do! Every time I minister to them, people out there get healed. I guess I have a healing anointing!" No, you don't, not yet anyway, but your pastor does.

You're in the development process. Will you at some point flow in the healing anointing? You probably will, but right this second, you do not.

"But I feel like I do." You don't.

"But I really feel like I'm called to that."

74

You are, but you don't.

I've had people say, "Well I'm called, I feel like I'm called to teach."

"And the servant of the Lord must not strive; but be gentle unto all men, apt to teach, patient, In meekness instructing those that oppose themselves; if God peradventure will give them repentance to the acknowledging of the truth."
- 2 Timothy 2:24-25

Notice it says that proper teaching will give God the opportunity to cause people to change their heart and mind. It didn't say the teaching would change their mind; the teaching would open the door for God to change their mind. It says a servant of the Lord is apt to teach. When someone comes to me and says, "Pastor, I have an anointing to teach. I know I'm called to be a teacher..."

First thing I may say is, "Go teach the kids."

"Well, I don't want to do that."

You're not apt to teach. What does "apt to teach" mean?
"I'll do it, I'll teach anybody, I'm apt to it!" See if you're apt to do something, you have a desire to do it. I would preach to a worm if you let me. I've preached to artificial trees in my house; I'll preach to anything. I don't care; one or one thousand, I'll preach. All people have character flaws, but the goal is to get you as fit as possible before we put you out there in ministry.

If you're supposed to be running a ministry and you don't show up, now everybody needs to shift positions to fill in for your absence. You're supposed to be in the kid's area, but you don't show up when you're supposed to, then you pretend to not know, "Oh, was I supposed to be in there?" Yes. You have a character issue. The staff at our church have ministry reports that are due every week. I can always tell who put thought into it. Some staff members write a novel on their report. That's good because they're thinking; I can tell. I read other reports, and if they have one word answers they're not thinking about their ministry or praying about their ministry. They're not asking God, "What do you want me to do?"

It's a lack of excellence. If you deal with people's soul and spirit in a sloppy way, do you think God is going to reward that or are you going to be held at a greater standard? What you do in excellence is ear-marked by the power of God that is vested in you! If you understand that you are anointed, then you will walk in your anointing and you will have excellence coming out of every pore. Everything you do will be excellent.

"Lord, who shall abide in thy tabernacle? Who shall dwell on thy holy hill? He that walketh uprightly, and worketh righteousness, and speaketh the truth in his heart. He that backbiteth not with his tongue, nor doeth evil to his neighbor, nor taketh up a reproach against his neighbor. In whose eyes a vile person is contemned; but he honoureth them that fear the Lord. He that sweareth to his own hurt, and changeth not."
- Psalms 15:1-4

You know what that means? You do what you say. You commit to it even if it costs you, even if it's to your own hurt. He says, "They don't change their mind." You can't lead a group of people if they're not willing to commit. Some have one foot in and one foot out. They're playing the hokey-pokey and they're turning themselves around, but they're not all-in with you. How can you build a ministry with people when they're not involved? You know when people are involved. When they are, you don't have to argue with them about arriving there on Friday night or arriving early on Sunday morning. They're begging, "Lord use me! Whatever I have I bring it to the table; use it as you wish! Even if it costs me money, I'm going to do it regardless of price because I said I'm going to do it. Even if I have to spend my time to do it, if I tell you I'm going to do it, I'm going to do it!"

When you call me, help comes. It's because I understand what I've been called to do. I am so glad that I kept my mouth shut in certain situations with my pastor. There were times he'd do something and I'd wonder, "What is he thinking?" But I said, "What do you need me to do boss?" Then it worked. The proof, as they say, is in the pudding.

Chapter Five:
The Art of Skill

There are too many people that are in ministry that should not be.. They are not ready to be in ministry because they do not have the skill set and/or they have not been through any training. I have pursued what I believe they call "higher education", but I'm just going to be honest with you. I'm extremely disappointed in the fact that, in some institutions, the education level (I believe) is not very high. As a matter of fact, it tends to be very low-level. It's scary because I'm finding that this is what's taught to future leaders. I often wonder, "How in the world is our future secured in the gospel?" The goal is obviously to train people to teach and spread the gospel. If Christ were going to do it all by himself, He would have done it. Therefore, He needs laborers. To be honest, it's very disappointing to see the material that is propagated and taught.

What I've come to realize is that, in some of the places that people have been raised up to teach the gospel, I don't know who taught them. When you sit in a classroom and watch how people respond to bad doctrine, you begin to wonder, "Where did they get trained and are they even trained?" When you hear a bad doctrine, the Holy Ghost should bear witness with you very quickly. You should be able to tell. It concerns and worries me that people don't know. I think it's because there are many poorly trained people that are functioning in the ministry and operating in callings they should not be in. Sometimes people have the misnomer that if they attend Bible College, that will license them in the ministry, but it doesn't. There are people I know that have been to Bible College that could not tell you anything about the Bible, and there are also those that have not been through schooling who could preach the paint off the walls while flowing in the Holy Ghost like you wouldn't imagine.

"Now when they saw the boldness of Peter and John, and perceived that they were unlearned and ignorant men, they marvelled; and they took knowledge of them, that they had been with Jesus."
-- Acts 4:13

We may think that meant they did not have manners, but it means they were not graduates of the recognized schooling structure. Yet, they could tell that they had been with Jesus because of the anointing that was on their life. It was discernible and not because of their educational background. Paul had a great deal of education. Remember that, by his education, he was a Pharisee. He was taught in all the best schools. Yet Paul said he counted it all as dung. With all his education as a learned Pharisee, he was still not usable by God until he had an experience on the road of Damascus. Then, Jesus began to unravel the heavenly vision of a purpose and a plan for him.

Was his education purposeful? Of course it is, all education is purposeful. It'll either teach you what to do or what not to do, so all education has value. It just depends on how you evaluate that experience.

You hear people say, "experience is the best teacher." That is not a truthful statement. There are people to whom I repetitively say the same things regularly. They've experienced me saying it, but yet they don't "get it". The saddest thing is to know the answer to the question, but yet be unable to articulate it. Experience does not do it alone; evaluated experience does. It's when you are able to look back at it and say, "Where did this come from? How did this happen and how do I keep it from happening again? God, what am I really supposed to get out of this?" Once you begin to evaluate your experience, then experience becomes fruitful in your life. Otherwise, you can keep going through the same problem over and over again.

It's dangerous not to be able to discern the things of God from the things of the flesh and to propagate information that is not biblical. The Bible says, that teachers are held to a higher standard. Realistically speaking, if it's not the right education, then it's all for nothing.

For example, I don't need a Doctorate to be "more anointed". The degree is something that the world recognizes, and it opens doors of opportunity. For that purpose, and that purpose only is there value. I think if you have a field in which you need specific training you would probably benefit from it. Realistically, the current day learning institution is a money-making business; an enterprise. If we don't understand the difference between what we need versus what people tell us we need, it can be dangerous. We have become a part of the world's system.

The subtly of understanding all of that comes with your ability to discern what is happening and what's not. The Bible does not tell you that you can't be "in the world", it tells you "do not be *of* it." Everything has a purpose and a place. Your ability to recognize that is absolutely critical. When you are looking to get into ministry, you have to make some decisions regarding your development and the commitment it requires.

"The Lord said unto Aaron, Go into the wilderness to meet Moses. And he went, and met him in the mountain of God [Horeb, or Sinai] and kissed him. Moses told Aaron all the words of the Lord with which He had sent him, and all the signs with which He had charged him. Moses and Aaron went and gathered together [in Egypt] all the elders of the Israelites. Aaron spoke all the words which the Lord had spoken to Moses, and did the signs in the sight of the people. And the people believed; and when they heard that the Lord had visited the Israelites, and that He had looked [in compassion] upon their affliction, they bowed their heads and worshiped."
-Exodus 4:27-31 AMP

Moses was very concerned about the ministry God had given him. God used Aaron to come alongside Moses to first and foremost help him interpret the call from God. If Aaron had received a different understanding from God than Moses,, then Aaron would have been justified in not going along with the plan. What Moses told Aaron bore witness with him because God had already prepared him. It was a divine relationship. As he walked with Moses, miracles were done, and confirmation followed.

We get wrapped up in these titles of "Bishops", "Apostles", "Chief Prelates" and "The Grand Poobah". What happened to checks and balances? If Moses heard it and he shared it with Aaron, now they can come together and ensure that everyone is hearing properly from God. You have people who claim they heard from God, but how come nobody else heard Him, as well? There tends to be people that are recognized in the church as elders or deacons- depending on your style of church. How come God did not speak to anyone else? The call on your life needs to be confirmed by someone close to you who understands how God moves. It's not a private calling. If it's not recognized, established, or endorsed by the church, you do not have a ministry. There is no higher office in the local church than the office of

82

a shepherd, so how could there ever be a ministry that was not sanctioned by a shepherd?

People called me "Pastor" way before I was one. They never met me and didn't know anything about me, but they would walk up to me and ask me, "Hey are you a pastor?" How would they know that if it were not divinely orchestrated in my life? I didn't choose the profession; the profession chose me. Thank God for it because I can't imagine someone doing this without the call or the anointing. People wonder, "Well, how come Pastor won't promote me?" In most cases it is not a denial, it is a delay. It is not a "No," it is a "Not now". I know the pain that you can experience by doing something you aren't called or anointed to do yet. Believe me, dealing with people and the challenges that come with them is not easy. Sometimes people will try to use you as their garbage can. It's easy with the anointing, but in the natural it's much more difficult. So what do I do? I protect people from spiritual failure.

"Well, I think I'm ready!" That's when you know you are not. If you think you are, then you know nothing as you ought to know it. Anybody that has half a brain is not rushing or jumping while shouting, "I just can't wait to get into ministry!" They understand what it really means. If you have an anointing, other people are supposed to confirm that you have one.

There's what is called the two-part giving of the Holy Ghost. The first is the spirit *within*, (the well on the inside of you), and it is where you draw your faith from. Then there is the spirit *upon*, (the river that flows through you) and that's the anointing for a service or it's used to accomplish a particular task pre-ordained by God. The river is not for you; it's for those around you. So it floors me sometimes when people say constantly, "Well I know my anointing," but no one else says anything. It's like you have a private river that no one else has access to. If you have a river that no one has access to, then what you have is a pond.

This next bit of information might save your life. I've seen people separate from their supply having decided that their ministry supersedes what God is doing in the local church. For example, one year our Kid's Ministry Leaders left because they didn't agree with the vision God gave me. That's equal to me walking into your home and saying, "I really don't like your couch right here." No one else will answer to God for the success of my ministry except me. You will answer for your commitment to what God has called you to do in this local body. Pass or fail, the responsibility of my ministry resides on my shoulders, a responsibility that I do not take lightly.

Interestingly enough, the mission of our kid's ministry is to develop and train the children, help them have relationships with their entire family, so the whole family begins to grow. They told me that was not what they wanted. This is why you have to ask yourself, "How are these people taught?" A week before they left, when confronted about this matter their response was, "We don't want to leave because the whole church will fall apart." My answer to that was, "Do not ever think this church is about you, because it's not." I could leave and the church wouldn't fall apart because it's not mine, it belongs to God. He has only given me stewardship over it. The ignorance that people hold fast to and accept as reality can be very dangerous.

"Then after fourteen years, I went up again to Jerusalem, this time with Barnabas. I took Titus along also. I went in response to a revelation and, meeting privately with those esteemed as leaders, I presented to them the gospel that I preach among the Gentiles. I wanted to be sure I was not running and had not been running my race in vain."
- Galatians 2:1-2 NIV

Fourteen years of ministry, training and pursuing development, by anybody's standard he would have been considered proficient. However, he received revelation and decided that he should talk to the ones who are esteemed as the leaders. He wanted to share his revelations to confirm that all that he was doing was not in vain. He was concerned that when his race was complete, he might find that what he had told everybody was in vain because it produced nothing.

I want to get to the end and know that I've accomplished something, that I produced fruit and God has seen it and is pleased of it. It is amazing to me how many people are running their race in vain. They appear to be moving fast, but they are not going anywhere. There's movement, yet no momentum.

When Paul and Peter had a disagreement they went to James, the acting pastor. Paul gave his side; Peter gave his side and then James listened and said, "Here is what we're going to do." If Paul was an apostle, why would he need to go to the pastor and ask him a question? James only wrote one book in the Bible, Paul wrote three quarters of the New Testament. Wouldn't we think it'd be the other way around?

My spiritual father will call me sometimes, even late at night, while traveling from one place to the other and he'll say, "Hey, listen to this," and he'll start telling me something that God shared with him.

Then he'll say, "Now all I want you to do is pray on it because I'm not going to teach it yet. I have to talk to a few people about it." Of course, he is not submitting to me as he is my spiritual father, but he still wants the counsel of the people he trusts. There are times where I will call him and I'll say, "Dad, what do you think about this?" He'll say, "Yeah, that's right on." Or, "No, that's not right," and help redirect my line of thinking.

There's a responsibility that comes with revelation. When people tell you, "God spoke to me and he told me thus and so," but nobody else heard it, you have to ask yourself, "Did God really speak?" If Satan can be the angel of light, then not all revelation is from God. Of course we have a more sure word of prophecy— we have the Word of God— but even after Jesus came out of forty days in the wilderness, Satan tempted him with scripture.

God will put divine relationships in your life and they are to counterbalance your personality. You may be zealous, but have no skill. You may be quick to jump and move, but you're not focused. God will put you with people who are designed to keep you within the proper boundaries until you have matured. The church should be the safe place; it is where you can be wrong, and Pastor will just come behind you and teach it the right way. He will bring correction or confirmation that will put you back on track. You will not be hurt by your mistakes. There's safety in the house; that's the purpose of it. Paul talked to the one regarded as the leader when he had his issue with Peter.

Everyone is subject to having a pastor. I don't care if you're the bishop, the pastor or the apostle; everybody should have a pastor, to someone whom they're accountable. When people are not held accountable, their doctrine becomes stale and old, and if it strays off there's no correction that can be made.

William Seymour was a one-eyed black preacher famous for the Azusa Revival. In those days, it was not permitted for a black man to be in a white school, so he spoke privately to Charles Parham about his desire to learn. Charles Parham allowed him to attend classes by opening the back door and allowing him sit out back. He could hear the class and the teaching, but couldn't gain entry. As William Seymour finished his schooling from that back door, he started what we know to be the Azusa Street Revival. In that revival, this man would put a chicken crate over his head, pray in tongues and the power of God would fall greatly. If you go to the location where the church was, there is a plaque posted from the city. They dispatched the fire department because the building appeared to be on fire, yet when they arrived nothing was consumed. The power of God resided so strong in his meetings that they thought the place was on fire, but nothing was burning. Charles Parham received news that there was some flesh stuff going on in those meetings, so he went to spectate. William Seymour learned from Charles Parham in his school. Now, Parham shows up and he sees some of the fleshly stuff and he knows it's in the flesh. When a move of God happens, Satan will always try to mimic that with a move of the flesh. Charles Parham wanted to deal with it but, unfortunately, Seymore did not agree and a sharp contention arose between them. It was not long thereafter the Azuza revival came to an end.

If my spiritual father came and told me that there is some flesh stuff in the church that needed to be dealt with, you know what I'm going to tell him? "We'll handle it!" He has full authority in our church. He doesn't have to ask if it's okay to lay his hands on people. He is my spiritual father, I've grown immensely in the things he has taught me. I know that my natural father would never come here and do harm towards me, and I know my spiritual father would never harm me. Do you know how many times Satan will try to turn me against him?

A move of God should have never been overthrown by the flesh, but Satan was able to quench it. I certainly don't agree with the segregation aspect of the story, but there were probably thousands of other black preachers that would have loved to sit in the back and listen.

When people hear submission, they don't hear protection; they hear control, hurt and abuse. If Charles Parham wanted to hurt William Seymour, he would have just done so. The flesh will always try to kill the move of God.

I've been in situations where I didn't understand what was going on and I thought to myself, "Why would my spiritual father do that? Is he trying to do that to hurt me?" Satan will respond with, "Yep. He's not for you; he's against you. You can do this on your own." No, I can't. Everybody must have a relationship with someone who can say to them, "You're wrong and this is not working." God used Jethro, Moses' father-in-law, to bring correction to him when he was trying to meet with all the people. God didn't send Aaron or his wife to talk to him; he used someone older and more experienced. People think they can just tell the pastor how things should be done in the church. If you want to correct and/or direct me, you better have an equal anointing or higher. God didn't use anybody under Moses to direct him, he used his father-in-law. God used Jethro to help Moses setup a hierarchy. When Moses did as he was instructed, it worked.

Yet, remember, when Aaron and Miriam decided they were going to tell him he couldn't marry the woman he wanted? Miriam ended up with leprosy. They thought that God spoke to them too. God responded and let them know that he spoke to them in dreams and visions, but to Moses, he spoke mouth to mouth. In other words, "I do not speak to him vaguely; I give him explicit instructions that are very clear." It is important to recognize that God gives the vision for his church to the pastor of each church. It not by committee, although committees may be used to provide counsel. The leadership is vested in the one that God has chosen and we have to be careful to honor and recognize that.

"Well God speaks to us too." Does He? He certainly can and will, however, we would do well to remember that the angel of light can also speak. I've watched people do things that they thought God told them to do. It brought harm to the church, but they did it anyway under the pretense that God told them to do it. Then, over time they are either no longer in church or they're hurt, not serving anymore and they're out of the will of God. Paul had fourteen years on the job but still decided to make sure he checked in with leadership so that his race was not in vain.

We have a society where people hop from church to church, looking for a ministry for the kids, but they look for the one that has theme park characters where the kids are appeased but not growing. Then the parents sit in the same place, and they're becoming dumbed down. It's so hard to tell people, "You're so focused on the job, but what would it mean to you if the world came to an end tomorrow?" Please don't get me wrong, I'm all about a job. Everybody needs to have an income. But when you allow the things in the world to turn you against the things of God, you really have to ask yourself, "What's going on and why?" because the spirit of the world has crept into the church.

Some are not interested in serving; they want commensurate pay for commensurate activity. "If I'm going to do anything, I want to be paid for it." Some, you could not even pay for their service. They don't want to take responsibility; they just want to be told what to do. Once you become a leader, you should -to some degree- know what to do; that's why you're a leader. You anticipate, prepare ahead of time, and understand what is going on in your life. Paul had revelation and wanted to present it to other leaders before he gave it to anyone else. That's leadership, forethought and planning ahead of time. If you believe you have a call to the ministry, you have to learn how to apply the things in this book to your life.

I mentioned in the last chapter Alexander the coppersmith and how Paul had said, "God will repay him." Earlier in Acts, Paul talked about Alexander and he said that he was teaching things and made shipwreck of the faith. The coppersmith began to teach things that were shipwrecking people.

Your decisions are not to be taken lightly. People have been changing churches as often as they change their attire. They pull away from the things of God as if it's "not a big deal" and then they attempt to operate with no skill level. They think there are no repercussions, but I assure you there are.

Find the church you're supposed to be at- if you're not there already. Wherever you're supposed to be planted is where God established the safety net for you until the ministry in you is perfected. Until then, you need to serve in the area of the need of the church until God develops the gift so that you can walk in your calling.

Chapter Six:
The Art of The Call

"And they said unto me, The remnant that are left of the captivity there in the province are in great affliction and reproach: the wall of Jerusalem is also broken down, and the gates thereof are burned with fire. And it came to pass, when I heard these words, that I sat down and wept, and mourned certain days, and fasted, and prayed before the God of heaven."
- Nehemiah 1:3-4

Throughout the Bible, you will see that when God called someone. He always called them either to a place, a task or to a life ministry. Nehemiah was called to a specific place. God began to reveal to him that which was going on in that particular area. It moved Nehemiah with such passion that he began to weep, mourn, and long for the success of the endeavors from those in Jerusalem. It compelled him beyond just having head knowledge to a place where he had a burning desire.

When God calls you to a place, He gives you a burning desire for that place. It is not just an understanding of social injustice— it is a deep-rooted, burning passion for a place that you cannot shake. It is so deep on the inside of you that it should move you beyond normal

91

human compassion. It puts a burden upon your heart that says, "This is something that I must do!"

People will think that they are called, but their first thought is, "It'll be cool to go to Africa!" There better be a burning in you that says you have to go because if you don't, you will step into a role that was not prepared for you and you may not find that out until you get there. If your not called to do something, and you go anyway, not only will you be doing yourself a disservice but you will be in a territory doing something you were never called to do, in a place that you were never supposed to be, with an anointing that you do not have. We need to be skillful with what God has given us, but the prevailing problem in the church is not sin, it's a lack of skill. Sin was dealt with 2,000 years ago. While it may be "cool" to travel and go see the world, I cannot tell you how much opposition you will run into. You will be ill-equipped because you think something is "cool". You'd better know, like Nehemiah; there was a burning in him that said, "I've got to deal with this, I cannot ignore it any longer. This is burning so deep on the inside of me that I need to do something about it." He was moved beyond just the normal realm of comprehension. That is a call. When he operated in his call, he was successful.

Noah was called for a task. God told him to build the ark. He wasn't called for a ministry, he was called for a specific task. In that day, people were mocking him. You have to know that people looked at Noah like he had lost his mind. As he is working away building the ark, people are wondering what he is doing. Imagine as he tells them that the great flood is coming and they're laughing at him, mocking him, and scorning because he is doing something that no one else has a clear revelation of. They didn't understand, but God had put a purpose in his heart. His wife was more than likely saying, "This is what we're going to do? We're going to put this in the back yard? We already have a car back here with no tires on it!"

If you haven't been called, you haven't had to fight for what you believe in with those that are closest to you. You can fight with people that do not know you, but when the people closest to you are the ones that become your enemies, you begin to realize you might be walking in a real call. The resistance will come from all angles. Noah was called to a task to build and construct that which would save the human race. He was the only one that truly understood it, yet the world was mocking him. However, there came a moment when they all said, "Uh-oh, you got room for one more?"

Since there's such a lack of understanding about the call, I don't think people realize how important or serious it is. I spend a lot of time preaching and teaching about the call to clarify with people their purpose and the way spiritual things function because I want everyone to understand what they are walking into. Elijah told Elisha, "You ask a hard thing". I have seen churches that have a total of ten people and five of them are pastors. How's that possible? Eph. 4:11 says that He gave *some*, not *all*. Somewhere along the line, people have not recognized that the call is not just a leader saying, "You're a pastor." You have to understand what you're about to walk into. Preparation and separation are required to ensure that you are equipped for the ministry you're about to walk in. I guarantee you, if you think it's a light task, you might not be called, but you're certainly deceived.

"Pastor, you know, I'm called to do thus-and-so!"

"Really?"

"I just can't wait!"

You'd be safer waiting, becoming skilled and learning how to deal with spiritual things. Right now you have the ability to make mistakes and somebody will speak into your life to help you make the adjustments. When you are out front and on your own, you don't have those luxuries anymore.

"But the Lord said unto him, Go thy way: for he is a chosen vessel unto me, to bear my name before the Gentiles, and kings, and the children of Israel: for I will shew him how great things he must suffer for my name's sake."
- Acts 9:15-16 KJV

Now we look at the Apostle Paul. God said He was going to show him the things that he must suffer, encounter, fight through and believe in Him through because He'll bring revelation of the gospel and teach people who they are in Christ."

The synaptic gospels of Matthew, Mark, Luke, and John are historical accounts of what has happened. The epistles that Paul wrote were written to explain why they occurred and what it means to you. Its one thing for me to articulate all of the details of history— and that's great; that's the historical account. However, it's a completely different matter when I'm able to tell you why it happened, what it means for your life, your salvation, and purpose. When I bring understanding to that which was hidden, I have now placed myself on the front line of an attack that Satan designed in order to keep you from ever knowing what your purpose and plan is. Everyone wants to know the answer to the age-old question, "What's my purpose in life?"

What is your purpose?

Your purpose is to serve God, bring the gospel to the lost and reflect Christ through your life. Satan does everything he can to disable, limit and blow out the tires on anything that seeks that endeavor.. Some concerning the call will rally around the idea of immovable faith. Touting "My God shall supply all my needs!" because we think the call is a call to comfort. It is not, it is a call to conflict. And we think, "I would love to be honored, regarded, respected and served! I just see the place where pastor sits and I would love to do that." If you think that way without counting the cost, you have missed it.

There are pastors who can preach the paint off the walls, but they are shutting down their churches at an alarming rate. People want the perceived honor and the position, but they do not recognize the problems and the challenges that come with it. God didn't tell Paul, "Hey I'm going to show you all the glorious exploits you're about to do. I'm going to show you that the lame will walk, and the blind will see and the deaf will hear." God told him that He was going to show him the things that he must suffer for the call. That's when you begin to realize that there is something different in you that is not alive in others.

You have to be careful not to judge others because you do not know what they have been through or understand the decisions they've had to make. I don't look at anybody's ministry and judge whether they deserve the success they have achieved. I did not walk in their shoes. I used to have soles put on the bottom of my shoes because I wore holes in them and I did not want anyone to know. The suits I had were separating; the material was fusing, separating and bumps were forming. I had to iron them right before I went to church and hope that I didn't sweat too hard, or it would start to bubble again. My first marriage became a satanic attack on my life in a way that I never thought would happen. I have lost houses and cars and honestly the list goes on and on. You don't know what people have had to go through; the fights they tolerated. People that were the closest to them, the ones they trusted and expected to support them, they had to fight them every day. Yet people judge.

"Well, how can he be a pastor and that happened?" I honestly don't know, but when you get the answer please let me know because I don't have all the answers, I just know what I had to go through. I think the better question is "Why did he remain a pastor after having gone through all of that?"

I've learned that I've gone through certain things because of the call that was placed upon my life. I'm not going to sit here and cry about it, I'm going to tell you it is, what it is. If you think that you have a call in your life, you had better understand there's a price that has to be paid. You may have to walk away from everything in your life in order to do what God has called you to do, but you must have enough fortitude and gumption to say, "I will do what God has called me to do regardless of what they say, what they think, what they feel, or what they think about me."

You'd better learn from somebody who is willing to invest something into you and teach you how to stand. I am grateful for the deposits that were made into my life. Being able to see from the back-end the things my pastor went through; how he stood up, preached fire, went into his office and about passed out. I am grateful. I watched people be healed in his ministry and then leave. They would come up for prayer, God would deliver them, and while they're in the parking lot they're talking crazy about him. I watched him go through that and that taught me to know that even when people's lives are changed, they'll still want to talk bad and go through the drama. I know that when I stand before God, He's not going to ask me about their walk. He's going to ask me about mine. I'm going to have to give an account for me and what I've done with what he's given me. The first thing you'll ever do if you decide to walk in the call God has for you is you'll run into conflict.

Does it get easier?

No, hate to break it to you.

Will you eventually be able to handle it better? Yes.

You will grow in your ability to cope and to overcome, but it doesn't ease up. The Greek word for *patience* is *hupomeno*. The word means "to live under". It is not the absence of pressure, but it is the presence of pressure that causes refinement, growth and change. If you do not want any pressure, then ministry is not for you. There will always be pressure.

Can you imagine having been told from the very beginning, that you're going to have to suffer through some things have some struggles and yet still having the presence of mind like Paul? If you can say anything about him, you have got to say that Paul was committed. God told him and showed him that he would have challenges, but he continued anyway. He knew that there was a cost to the call, and his call was not to comfort; it was a call to conflict. Isn't that amazing? He stayed with it, he stuck to it and he didn't give up.

It's so difficult to spell out to people how great the call is. It's wonderful and every one of you are called for a purpose, a task or a place. You're called for something, but I want you to understand that it's no light thing. People have put away the call for the world, the job, the school, the family; for everything other than the call itself, and never realized that the eternal purposes in their life are not from the things of this world. Paul was skilled at persecuting and killing Christians. How in the world could this man stand before King Agrippa and say, "I have not been disobedient to the heavenly vision?" God finally brought him the clarity and the revelation that said, "Now that I've got you trained, this is what I need you to do." Do we ever consider that God knew Paul was going to kill Christians and people's lives were at stake? This man was being developed whether he knew it or not, and God used Paul to write 75% of The New Testament.

Knowing what you have to go through doesn't make going through it any easier. To be honest with you, I'd rather not know, let it surprise me. At least I won't have to deal with the agony. It's like getting a beating from your parents. When they call you and say, "I'm going to whoop you when I get home," now you're staring at the clock. "I know it's coming…" The call has to be taken seriously and there's a price that has to be paid. God needs to know, before He gives you a closet full of suits and shoes, can you be faithful with the one suit you have now?

Some of you see things that other ministers have and by comparison begin to desire them. You don't have any clue the price they had to pay to walk in their calling. The sad part is in some ways; most people do not care. All they want to do is critique. "Ignorance gone to seed" is when the world begins to say things like "I don't know why they're always giving all their money, that's why Pastor looks so sharp." No, let me help you understand something. Pastor dresses the way he dresses because he was faithful when he didn't have enough. It had nothing to do with you. People don't understand the things you have to go through. No one understands the houses I've had to give up or the businesses I've had to let go of. You don't know what it's like to have the call be the center of your life. How would you like the very person who confessed that they would spend the rest of their life with you— the one who convinced you to start a church that you didn't want to start because you were afraid of them—to get four years into it, and then they decide they don't want to do it anymore? Now you have souls who are dependent upon you, looking at you, and now you are faced with the disgrace and the potential shame of the idea that you now have to walk away from an institution that you so vehemently preach about. You don't know the cost of the call, it's not something to be played with and it's not easy, but it's necessary. Then, you watch God move anyway. You think to yourself "It's over."

What happens when you are praying with everything you have and you feel God is not saying anything? You struggle because you wonder, "What will people say? How do you recover from this? What are your fellow ministers going to say about you? How will they judge you? Will they label you? How will the congregation respond? Will they abandon you?" If they were going through it, they'd expect me to be there and stay with them side-by-side. They'd expect me to be by the hospital bed, to pull closer to them and inject them with the Word and build their faith to the place where they could stand on their own. But what happens when you have to do that for yourself?

You wonder if you've been taught well enough and if you have enough in you. You wonder, "If I had an anointing, why is this happening? Why am I going through this? Why when I pray and pray, binding and rebuking demonic attack against my spouse, which I should have authority over, why is it not working?" But still, you go and preach to everyone and tell them that you can have authority in God when you cannot get it to function for yourself.

There are some realities of this walk with Christ when you decide, "I'm not going to preach these feel-good, 'Fuzzy Wuzzy was a bear, Fuzzy Wuzzy had no hair' messages." We are in a season where this thing is wrapping up. If you have any natural discernment whatsoever, you should be able to look into the world and see that the end is near, whether or not its tomorrow, five years from now, a hundred years from now, I do not know. God needs laborers to come up out of their comfort zone and make a decision for Christ and say, "I'm going to do what God has called me to do and I'm going to do it until the wheels fall off. I'd rather they laugh at me for serving God than to laugh at me because I failed."

D.L. Moody is quoted saying "God never called a lazy man." People are lazy about the things of God. It shows in how you sweep the floor, or anything else that you've ever been asked to do for the ministry. A person walks in the door, they come and hear a great message but then they walk into the lobby and a greeter gives them the evil eye. They will walk out that door with the thought in their head, "Those people are mean." I don't care how good the message was, don't care how much the anointing fell, one person can trip somebody up. They can walk into the bathroom, kid's rooms or sanctuary, see it in poor condition and think, "Wow, they have no respect for their own place." One thing can affect people in a negative way. God never calls a lazy man.

You cannot be spiritually lazy. You have to understand that if there's a calling upon your life, then you have a requirement to bring your best to the one who gave His best. What if God had said, "I'm not giving my son, but I'll give my dog"? He gave the best of what He could give and He gave it all! Jesus didn't fall short; He put everything on the line! How dare we ever think that all is not required! He doesn't want half; He wants all of it, but we've learned through school and work that we can "get by" on talent, so we don't bring everything; we just bring enough. If you feel your call can be walked out with your talent alone, then you are not called. Paul said, "I press toward the mark for the prize of the high calling of God." That meant it was an aspiration, a dream or a requirement that was beyond himself. It was high, it was difficult and it looked impossible. If you can do it by yourself and fulfill it within your own abilities; if you can wrap your mind around it and figure it out, it is not your calling. Your calling will always be something that perplexes you. It should scare you; it should not look possible and it will frighten you from the top of your head to the soles of your feet! You should be afraid of how people will respond to it. It's like your testimony. Some of you have a practiced testimony, the one that you tell everybody. "Oh, I remember one time I needed some money..." but you don't tell anyone about the things you've really gone through. I am talking about the moments when you didn't know what God was going to do, if He would even do it, and you weren't even sure that God existed.

"They were on the way going up to Jerusalem, and Jesus was walking on in front of them; and they were bewildered and perplexed and greatly astonished, and those [who were still] following were seized with alarm and were afraid. And He took the Twelve [apostles] again and began to tell them what was about to happen to Him."
- Mark 10:32

When you're the leader, you're the one that is hit first because you're out in front. You will know about things before others will

100

know about them and sometimes you can see an attack coming before it hits. That's why you're being trained and taught. If you can't take my criticism, and my criticism comes because I love you and want to help you, wait until you're criticized by people in public who don't love you. You tell people to make an adjustment and they're mad for days, storming out the door. What happens when you really have to fight, when it's all you? What happens when there is no one around to tell you, "Hey listen, you might want to fix that."

Jesus was out front and the leader always takes the hit before everybody else does. You have no idea the pressures that you have to withstand and still preach with a smile on your face - throwing in a joke every once in awhile so people don't get too mad at you. Yet and still you're under attack and harassed. Every demon in hell that comes after you comes after your leader because if they can knock the head off first, everyone will fall and that's his plan. I often compare Satan to a sniper. He's not always a uni-bomber. We think he comes in and tries to blow up everything. He's trying to take out leadership. That's why there are those of you that are involved in the church and as soon as you decided to step up to leadership your life went upside down. Why? You made a commitment to the call.

Some have made a commitment to answer the call, but they are not as faithful as they need to be. Now you are fighting at a level that you don't want to step up to, because there is a lack of discipline. You're wondering why the struggle is there, but it's hold stays because you will not step up to the level of which you said yes to the call. The moment you said, "yes" to the call, you've answered the summons. Once you've answered the summons, you are no longer among the regulars. You can no longer be spiritually lazy. God does not call the lazy. Now you have to operate at a higher level.

Notice something, the apostles were perplexed, alarmed, afraid and astonished. Jesus is telling them, "I'm going to go to die." It is not the call that will qualify you; it is your ability to stay connected to the one who's responsible for your soul that will. You can follow and still be afraid and perplexed, but if you let your inability to understand pull you away, then you'll follow no more. They weren't sure; they were scared, but they followed anyway. Most assuredly if Jesus said, "They're going to kill me", what would the natural assessment be? "They're going to kill us too!" Yet they followed anyway.

My mom used to say this to me all the time, "The older I get, the less I know." When I was young I thought I knew everything, had all the answers and at times I thought she was crazy. What she meant was that the more experience she gets, all the things that she counted as, "This is the way it's supposed to be", was all flipped upside down.

The older I get, the more I realize this life we live is not everything I thought it was supposed to be. God doesn't do everything in a neat little box the way that I expected him to do it. Sometimes my answer comes in what I think is my denial, and what I believe to be my delay is actually my answer. I've learned not to put God in a box, to not judge other people and not to put myself in a place where I critique what everybody else is doing. I am not going through what they're going through and I have learned that situations can change in the blink of an eye. Your life can be flipped upside down, everything can change and there is only one thing that is of surety and that's the rock; his name is Jesus Christ! Everything else is subject to change and everyone else is subject to leave.

"[Saying] Behold, we are going up to Jerusalem, and the Son of Man will be turned over to the chief priests and the scribes; and they will condemn and sentence Him to death and turn Him over to the Gentiles."
- Mark 10:33

Can you imagine the fortitude it took for Jesus to say, "I know what I need to go through, and I was created for this purpose. I know the attack and the criticism I'll deal with, but I was made for this moment and everything in my life was building up to it. All the situations and circumstances were shaping me for the moment where I'll go to the cross and not even be recognized. I will be beat within an inch of my life and killed. I've been battle-tested and proven for that day. Everything has been to equip me to be what God has called me to be, which is why I am able to stand here in front of you and say, 'If you follow me, I might be persecuted, spit on, attacked— It might be my death, but I am still willing to go because I don't have another answer."

I have one answer and His name is Jesus Christ. I don't have anything else. Some of you have other options and I'm proud of you, but I do not. Sometimes my blind following is not out of my preponderance of faith, but it's out of my lack of choice. Sometimes tenacity comes from a lack of options. Take it how you want, but I would not trade it for the world. I can certainly identify with Peter when he said that he had nowhere to go and that Jesus had all the answers to eternal life.

I did trade it for the world, and I came to the understanding I could no longer live that way and I had to birth what God had put in me. It was something in me that was shut up in my bones, it just moved me to the place where I was weeping for people I had never met. I was believing God to teach people that I'd never seen and believing in a flow and anointing that I'd never walked in before. I was believing and seeing what has now come to pass and will continue to do so.

Did it scare me? Yes.

Was I afraid? At times, yes.

But I knew God had to do it because within me was no ability to accomplish it. I guarantee you, some of the disciples did not agree with it, but Jesus asked Peter, "Will you leave me?" He said, "We don't have any other answers. You're the one with keys to eternal life." Once you found it, where else can you go? What else can you turn to? When

THE ART OF FOLLOWING

you know the truth, what else can you do? You already know the truth, you've reached the crescendo, you are on the tipping point; you now know what everyone else in the world is dying to figure out. Where else can you go?

"For we would not, brethren, have you ignorant of our trouble which came to us in Asia, that we were pressed out of our measure, above strength, insomuch that we despaired even of life: But we had the sentence of death in ourselves, that we should not trust in ourselves, but in God which raiseth the dead..."
- 2 Corinthians 1: 8-9

There were things that some of us had to go through in order for God to create greater commitment in us;otherwise we would not have become involved or gone any deeper in the things of God. Your comfort did not bring commitment; your comfort brought complacency. "Somebody else will do it." or, "You know, I'll get around to it. You don't understand; I'm busy. I have stuff to do. I mean, this is not everything for me." That's too bad; because when everything comes to an end and you stand before God, He's not going to ask you, "How'd you do at your job? What kind of grades did you get in school? What happened to the cars, the money and all the stuff? Did you enjoy it all? Was it fun?" He's going to ask you, "What did you do with what I gave you? Were you a wise steward of your time, your treasure and your talent? Were you a wise steward of the things I've blessed you with?"

We have to keep the main thing, the main thing. Paul said the reason they were pressed out of their measure is so they would be forced to trust in God. It's bizarre how when most people come into conflict and they're perplexed; they walk away instead of going deeper in their commitment. Like Paul said, the ones that were following, they continued to follow. They were perplexed, they were afraid, their lives were in jeopardy. They were not sure what the outcome's going to be, but still, they followed. You can change a city with people like that, and affect the whole world. There's a group that will grow fearful and walk away, but there's a group of believers that will be afraid and stay with it. Even if they're warming their hands at the enemy's fire now, God still has a plan and purpose for them. Isn't that amazing?

"This is a true saying, If a man desire the office of a bishop, he desireth a good work."
- 1 Timothy 3:1 KJV

Notice he said, "If you desire the office, you desire a good work." He goes on to outline the requirements of what the bishop and deacons need to be then tells us, "Test them, make sure." If you think they're a deacon, if you think they're in the office of a bishop, test them. See how they'll respond because that'll tell you if they're ready. Few understand that a lot of times, leaders are testing people to see if they're ready. Sometimes I hear the right answer and sometimes I see the wrong one. The Bible tells us to test you before you get put into ministry because you will need a strong character to pair with your anointing.

Elijah threw the anointing on Elisha; the mantle was on him. Elisha's head could have swelled up (figuratively). 1 Timothy 3:6 tells us to make sure that we're careful about recent converts because they can get prideful and Satan will take them out. Elisha had the anointing. Elijah threw it on him, didn't he? The mantle's now on him. in 1 Kings 19:16, God told Elijah to do what? "Invite him into thy room." Why? To show him how to use the mantle that was put on him. What if Elisha said, "You know what, I'm not going to follow you. I have the anointing now so I can just go." If he had said that, that same anointing that was thrown upon him would eventually lead to his undoing because he'd be unskillful with it.

Some people do have an anointing; it's already on them. The leaders job is not to give you a greater anointing; they are not able to do that. It's God who calls. Their responsibility is to help you become skillful in what you're about to walk into.

The leader's responsible for your safety, your protection, and to tell you what you need to hear so that you can grow- to get you off the milk and into the meat. However, if you can't take a course correction by one who loves you, what happens when you get course-corrected by the one who hates you? A pilot makes course corrections to the plane. He has a vested interest in its success so when he makes a course correction, it eventually lands in the right airport. When Satan makes a course correction; you'll experience earthquakes, storms and problems. When that plane crashes, majority of the people on board are now dead. Which course correction do you want? Do you want the instruction of a skilled pilot, or do you want the one by the world that causes death? I guarantee you if you won't be corrected, Satan will love to steal the opportunity to correct you mid-flight. I believe there are so many people that are called, and the call of God on your life is something that is to be revered. It's to produce awe in you, inspire you, motivate you, and drive you. It should be like fire in your bones and you just can't deny it. But guess what I'm going to need you to do— contain it. Become skilled with it, learn the things you need to learn so that when you may have to stand all by yourself, you'll be able to stand. David said in Psalms that his tears have been his meat day and night, but he encouraged himself.

The people wanted to stone David; they wanted to kill him. They came home from battle and the enemy took their wives and their children! They wanted to kill David. He could not turn to them and say, "Hey, encourage me." There's a point as a leader where you have to get out front and you're going to have to encourage yourself. When nobody else knows what else to say, you have to know what to say. You need to have that relationship with the One who created you, the

One that is on the inside of you, because sometimes that is the only relationship you will have. It's by design that we're lead into conflict, not comfort, to produce commitment. Some have become way too comfortable. You have it all down to a science, all figured out to the point where it's on auto-pilot. It is a sure-fire sign that it might not be your call because you will never get your call under control. It's not possible.

"Not a novice, lest being lifted up with pride he fall into the condemnation of the devil. Moreover he must have a good report of them which are without; lest he fall into reproach and the snare of the devil. Likewise must the deacons be grace, not double-tongued, not given to much wine, not greedy of filthy lucre; Holding the mystery of the faith in a pure conscience. And let these also first be proved; then let them use the office of a deacon, being found blameless. Even so must their wives be grave, not slanderers, sober, faithful in all things. Let the deacons be husbands of one wife, ruling their children and their own houses well."
- 1 Timothy 3:6-12

Prior to that, it says if a deacon can't rule in his own house, how can he rule in the house of God? Notice, he says the deacons and their houses need to be right.

Years ago,when I would hire lower level sales person or a general level employee, I didn't really care about their spouse per se. However, when I was hiring a Vice President, a President or a Director level employee, my interview process included meeting their spouse. Why? I need to see if they're supportive, or crazy. I need to put them in a relaxed environment to see how they respond. What do we do? We do not go to the office; we go to dinner; let your guard down and see how many drinks you order. See, it's universal. Why is it important? If you're yoked up with someone who can't support you, someone who's going to hurt you, then ultimately it's going to hurt your ministry.

There are some callings where you're going to have to have somebody to help and support you.

You have to check everybody. Everybody's got to be on the same page. Some of you, this is the roadblock to your promotion in ministry. It might not have anything to do with you, sometimes it's the person you're yoked up with- or the person you're not yoked with. The calling on your life is greater than your life.

You don't know the tears I've shed. You don't know the times I've been on my knees begging God, "Seriously God? Really? Why don't you just kill me? I do not want to do this. Your people are like herding cats." You know what they say; dogs have masters and cats have staff. You do not know the countless times that God has woken me up in the middle of the night to pray for one of the flock. I do not know what you're doing, or why you're doing it, I just know God told me, "Pray." Would you not be upset if I told you I'd just roll over and went back to sleep?

There's a call in your life and if you sense it, I want you to be skillful with it. I want you to count the cost because there is a price that has to be paid and it could cost you everything. I guarantee you that a man who stands for nothing will fall for anything. You have to be able to recognize and discern there are times you will have to stand when no one else will and speak up when no one else will talk. There might be a place that you're called to, it might be a task that you're called to, or it might be a life-long ministry that you're called to, but whatever it is, let's get busy about it.

In the movie *Shawshank Redemption*, the main character, Andy, said, "I'm either going to get busy living or get busy dying." We only have two choices; to do, or not. What is your choice? If they're going to mock you, laugh at you and talk about you, let them do so because you're serving God. Let them talk about you because you're committed to something higher than yourself, you're at church on

Sunday instead of "getting your swerve on" Saturday night. You stand for something and you're willing to represent the Christ in you, the hope of glory!

Let it be something that is worthwhile so God will see your persecution and say, "They have stood up for me. They have not denied me in front of men and I will not deny them." If there are things that your leader teaches that you don't like hearing, your character needs help. If they start going down a certain avenue and you're like, "Oh God, here we go..." your character needs help. Never forget this one truth; your anointing will open doors for you, your gift will bring you before kings and your character will keep you there. Wait until those who hurt you behind closed doors become mad enough to hurt you in public. No surprise to you, you've been hurt in private for way to long- so when the public expression is no shock to you. It shocked everybody else, but no shock to you. Wait until you have to go through that. You need to have a strong character to sit there and let somebody throw dirt at you, say everything bad about you; all the while keeping your peace.

He said there's nothing wrong with desiring the office. You desire it; that's a good thing. You should want the call that's in your life; that's a good thing. I'm not sharing this information to make you afraid of your call. What I'm trying to do is to help you be sober about it. Some of you are like drunk little kids. "I can't wait 'til I get up there! If Pastor just gave me an opportunity, boy I'll get up there, I'll preach the paint off the walls! They just don't know!" Yeah, right. Wait until all hell breaks loose in your home because you want to get up and preach, then we'll see how that all works.

There is a price to be paid for the call. Pay it, because it's the best decision you'll ever make. Stop trying to put it on layaway. Stop trying to avoid the phone calls from the bill collectors, pay it! Some of you want it in the blink of an eye. I served for eight years under my pastor, carried his bags, went everywhere he went, heard all of his messages. I was the one shouting him down, trying to keep him encouraged, driving him everywhere he needed to go. At times, I paid for his travel expenses so he could go preach. That way, he could keep all the money for himself and not have to struggle. I brought my supply for eight years and you want it in one. It does not come overnight, it does not come because you want it bad. It comes because you end up in conflict, which produces commitment.

I know people that have gone through more problems than a little bit. They still have no character and that's why they're still in problem after problem. Problems don't produce character, it reveals character. You have to know that you can stand and if you're not sure that you can stand, that's why you're in the church. Trust me, by the time I get through with you, you'll be able to stand because I won't let you fail. Some people when they say they're going to help you, they show up, but they're not there to help you. You better believe when you ask me to come help you that help actually just showed up. You better believe that I'm going to bring everything I can, to make sure that I've helped you because it's my name, reputation and anointing on the line. In some ways, I am very concerned with how people view me, but they don't care how I view them. The moment they get what they want; they're gone. I did not do it for them anyway; I did it for God. Why? Because I take the call very seriously!

Chapter Seven:
The Art of Honor

"Let nothing be done through strife or vainglory; but in lowliness of mind let each esteem other better than themselves."
- Philippians 2:3

You have to ask yourself, as some of the great generals of the faith have gone home to be with the Lord, why is it that very few have been raised up to take their place? It's always a common discussion when a minister passes away, especially one of the well-known ones. Someone always says, "I wonder who will get their anointing." That becomes a topic around the dinner table among ministers and sometimes in fellowship they'll ask, "I wonder whose going to get this person's anointing?" We don't realize or recognize that it is not up to that individual as to who gets their anointing; it's about those who followed them.

One of the challenges that I believe people face today is a lack of honor. A lack of honor pertains to a lot of things that are not just ministry related per se, it also deals with relationships and business. If you're in a relationship or business and you are around people that have a lack of honor, it shows. Honor does a tremendous amount of good towards the success of a relationship, just as much as the

111

antithesis of honor, familiarity, will destroy a relationship, and it is bred in so many different ways.

The first thing that we have to recognize is that honor is not a feeling- it's an action. I can tell you that I love you and I care about you, but if I display no love or care towards you then I do not honor for you. In the same way, people think love is an "ooey-gooey" feeling, but love is something that requires a commitment. It's easy to love somebody when they're dressed their best, but it gets harder when you wake up next to somebody and they look totally different than when you went to sleep.

We have allowed the world to define relationships, roles and genders because we've allowed the world to change how God designed things. When one has honor towards another, you esteem them better than you.

As I've traveled with my spiritual father, I've watched how other ministers have dealt with him and I watch how I interact with him. Others, they just want to hang out and be invited. I've told my spiritual father this and I meant it; I said, "I'm not your friend, I love you, you're my dad and I want to be a son. I don't want to be your friend." I have too much honor for him.

Once you start hanging out, now you want to go fishing and golfing together, but you forget the original nature of the relationship. When you esteem people better than yourself, then you don't see yourself on the same level as they are. I don't see myself on the same level as he is because he has way more years of experience in the ministry, but to be honest with you even if he did not have more experience, he still has a greater anointing. The Bible instructs us to know no man after the flesh. I seek to fellowship with him around the things of the spirit.

When I first entered into real estate I was eighteen years old. I was selling millions of dollars in real estate. My counter-parts (who were significantly older than me) would always comment, "Where does this kid think he came from?" I didn't come from anywhere; I'm just willing to work and work hard. I used to wear a wedding ring on my finger so that people would think that I was much older than what I was. I always carried myself as being older, but I understood the principles of work, and I worked hard. I had one lady come up to me in the real estate office, she said, "Who do you think you are that you have an assistant?" I'm real quick with the wit because I looked at her said, "Remember if you don't have an assistant, then you are one." Then I walked away. Now she was certainly calling me all kinds of names, but that's not my problem. I'm the type of person where I'll work hard to get what I want. If I want it then I'm going after it and I'll give it everything, I have. What I realized is that they had issues with me because of my age and I've struggled with that, for the most part, all of my life professionally. In the church, people look at me and ask, "Well how old are you?" Sometimes in my head I want to say "None of your business!" Either I have an anointing, or I don't. It seems that when people ask that they are setting me up to be dismissed and/or disqualified over my age. Call it what you want, but the challenge is this; The Bible tells us to know no man after the flesh. It doesn't matter their age, what matters is their anointing. If they have a greater degree of an anointing, then they are worthy of honor, but people are taught in today's society to dismiss honor.

There used to be a time where a little kid would not talk to you without saying, "Sir" or "Ma'am." Nowadays, you're liable to be cussed out by a four-year-old and then they'll look at you like you've lost your mind. That's the society that we live in. The world has gained influence in the church and thusly there is very little honor. Just about every TV show, from cartoon to sitcoms, will portray that the wife is the hero in the house, the man is an absolute idiot who receives zero honor and the kids are smarter than both of them combined. I am not sure if that is art imitating life or if life is beginning to imitate art. Personally I believe it is the latter because I was never smarter than my parents. I could think ahead to my fastest moment and they'd be sitting there waiting for me. I don't know how it all happened,, but society has created this problem.

When you see a wife that's submitted to her husband, she becomes the butt of jokes. That is sad because I do not care which translation of the Bible you read, a wife is told to honor her husband and the husband is told to love his wife. In honor comes love for a man and if a man loves his wife he will honor her. When the man, becomes too familiar, he no longer "hung the moon" and he can tell because he's treating like he's not that guy that he used to be. All of a sudden he's the fix-it guy, the "honey-do."

People who are selfish have a hard time with honor because they always feel it's not necessary, it's too much, and it's a narcissistic viewpoint. "That's just too much. You know they put their pants on one leg at a time just like I do." I beg to differ. I put my pants on both legs at a time.

Honor is "to have high respect for worth, merit or rank". I can always tell who has honor for me and who does not. I never say anything, I just avoid them. I do not put my time into them; I will not answer their phone calls, or respond to their messages when I know they do not have honor for me. They don't call me "Pastor Gene", in their minds I'm "Gene". Here's the problem; "Gene" may not like you, yet Pastor Gene loves you; he would give his life for you and be there in a New York second. If you need some help, you can call Pastor Gene and he will be there. When I show up, help comes with me, guaranteed. Gene, on the other hand, would rather go fishing.

The way that you approach someone will be indicative of the supply that you receive from that person. With my spiritual father Reverend Ricky, I do not need "Ricky". As a matter of fact when "Gene" and "Ricky" get together it's really not good, we love to kid. But one thing's for sure, when I recognize the supply that's in him then

114

I receive so much that you could not buy it, it's intangible. There's no way you could quantify it because I recognize his supply is for me. Being able to maintain the proper boundary is an art all unto itself.

In Nancy Dufresne's message titled *"The Role of Music"*, she talks about how she was preparing to buy her son a drum set. Someone told her the following (I am paraphrasing) "Don't buy him a cheap one. If you buy him a cheap one and he learns how to play on that then his ear will become accustomed to it and it'll ruin his ear. Then, when you want him to graduate to a good one, he won't know the difference." When I hear my spiritual father talking to me, I do not care what he's saying or how he says it, I am tuned into making sure that I hear all that I need out of what is being said. When you look at the messenger then you begin to say, "Well how come he couldn't have said that a little nicer?" It may not be part of his personality, plain and simple. If you want something from them, you better learn how to deal with their personality; their style. When he says things to me in a way that could have rubbed me the wrong way- you know how they say if you're rubbing the cat the wrong way, turn the cat around? That's what I do; I turn it around. I make sure that I receive the message. Why? I esteem him higher than myself.

What we have learned, unfortunately through the infiltration of Satan, is that he would exalt his throne as God's. One of Satan's first goals was to elevate himself above God. Familiarity is easily spotted by the overwhelming desire to escalate your position with everyone. "Pastor and I hung out, so you know, that's Gene now."

All of a sudden, somewhere along the line we've leveled ourselves out in our position which is why I have to be very careful with people because next thing you know, you'll come tell me some crazy stuff that I am not interested in, nor do I care, nor do I want to know because you've shifted the relationship.

We have to be very careful to discern the relationships in our lives and understand how divinely orchestrated they are. The Bible says to esteem each other better than yourself because I guarantee you, strife and vainglory will always step in when you do not esteem other people. I do not care if my spiritual father called me every name in the book. You cannot get offended at that which you honor. The only time you can get offended is when you have expectations in your heart that you deem unfulfilled. "This is how this is supposed to be done. This is what he's supposed to see in me. This is how this person, man or woman, is supposed to treat me."

Once you have preconceived expectations, honor becomes very difficult for you. I've had people who struggle with the way people honor me or do not honor me and it's a lack of submission, it's a heart issue. If you cannot honor the man you do see, you're not going to honor the God you can't see. This is where people struggle immensely. Now, I'm not talking about hero worship and I'm not talking about putting man on a pedestal, I'm talking about recognizing the office in which the man stands in. The only thing that is put on a pedestal is a statue, and they're usually getting pooped on by pigeons.

I listen more than I talk when I'm with my spiritual father. What am I doing? I'm taking notes; I'm listening and growing. If he's in a certain type of mood, I'm in the same mood. "You don't want to talk? I don't want to talk. As soon as you are willing to talk I'm willing to listen." I understand the divine nature of the relationship. If iron sharpens iron, then I need to recognize where my supply comes from. In that, I am not bringing strife; I'm shooting down all strife. Any time there's anything related to strife, I'm trying to figure out how to fix it. I'll give you a very practical example.

He needed to get a haircut, but he was on the phone with someone because there was a problem back at the church. I'm riding in the car with him. I could have sat there, waited and let him figure out where to have his haircut, but I picked up my phone, used my map program, found three places and I called them- all while he's still on the phone. I found which ones were available, and when he got off the phone I said, "You're already booked in there, ready to go. They're waiting for you." We show up, and it's done. He and I aren't equals. I'm not sitting there thinking, "He can figure it out on his own; it's his head," because I honor him. I didn't sit there and say, "I'm in the ministry like he is." No, I recognize his office, who he is and what he means to me because you display value toward that which you honor. Vice versa, when you don't display or put any honor on someone, you are actually letting them know that you despise them.

Jesus replied, "And why do you, by your own traditions, violate the direct commandments of God? For instance, God says, 'Honor your father and mother,' and 'Anyone who speaks disrespectfully of father or mother must be put to death.' But you say it is all right for people to say to their parents, 'Sorry, I can't help you. For I have vowed to give to God what I would have given to you.' In this way, you say they don't need to honor their parents. And so you cancel the word of God for the sake of your own tradition."
-Matthew 15:3-6 NLT

He's saying that if you really honor your mother and father, then you would not withhold gifts from them. Honor is not a measure of your lip-service, but a measure of your actions. Here's the thing, it never said, "Honor your mother and father because they were a great mother and father", you honor them because they gave birth to you, plain and simple. "Well I don't think they deserve it." You don't deserve honor either. They are still your mother and father. We have, as a society, developed a mindset where we want to do what is right in our own eyes, so we measure whether honor is due based on if we think they earned it. The problem with earning honor is that it is subjective to the one who displays the honor.. Bestowing honor is not based on whether you think they earned it, deserve it, or are worth it. It is done because it is a commandment of God based on their position. Jesus said that honoring your parents is not an option. It's the first commandment with promise that if you honored your mother and father, so shall your days go well.

It is so appalling to watch people that will honor their children more than their spouse. You're honoring the creation over the creators. Spiritually, we recognize that if God gave you something, that's the creation and we worship the creator, but I've heard women say, "My kids come before my husband." So when he comes home, he can't even get the big piece of chicken? "Well, he'll just have to wait!" How did we get there? That's not scriptural. Of course, I understand where sacrifices should be made for the sake of the children but what I am addressing is the blatant demotion of a man to a second- class citizen in his own home.

"Honor the Lord with thy substance, and with the firstfruits of all thine increase: So shall thy barns be filled with plenty, and thy presses shall burst out with new wine."
-- Proverbs 3:9-10

My pastor would say he needed a TV and what people would do is go out and buy a new TV for themselves and they would give him their old TV. I never did that. If he needed something and I knew he needed it, particularly if I bought me a new TV then I bought him a new one too. If he needed something and I bought it for me, I bought him one too. I bought a four hundred dollar fountain for my office and his office. If I couldn't afford two then I bought one for him and I asked him for his leftovers. Why did I do that?

I honored him, but we tend to do things by our lips and not by our actions. It's easy to say, "Oh my pastor, I love my pastor!" The moment he does something people don't understand and or like, all of a sudden it's time to move on. I don't get excited about people that come to our church for the first time and say, "Oh Pastor that was the greatest message I ever heard! It spoke right to me!" Next Sunday comes and they're nowhere to be found. It's usually the ones that don't say anything that come back. Your actions will always speak louder than your words.

The Bible says, "Honor the Lord with the first fruits of thy increase and honor the Lord with your substance." That takes honor beyond "talking about it" to "being about it". God says that when you honor in that way, so shall your barns be filled with plenty and your presses shall burst with new wine. That speaks to enterprise. A wine press was used for enterprise. Many years back I had three companies going at the same time, I was serving in the church and I was teaching in Bible College. I understood that if I wanted the businesses to function with minimal effort from me, then I had to learn how to honor with my substance. As long as I did that, more came.

Some of you are trying to figure out how to fix your financial problems by natural means and it is not possible. If you would bring your first fruit, which is your tithe, and learn how to honor God with your substance, The Bible tells us that he will give you buildings that you did not build and vineyards that you did not plant. How is that possible? It is by the spirit, but you have to give honor. A lack of honor in the area of our finances and substance is one of the major reasons why some people get blessed and some people do not. Once you get that, you'll never want for anything ever again. If you do not have it, the supply of the one whom you honor will have it. In the same way, if you honor God with your tithe then when you don't have enough, knowing that you are in covenant with Him, then what is His is yours. That's why He said, "I'll give you vineyards you didn't plant, I'll give you houses you didn't build," because it all belongs to Him. Once you understand honor and you recognize Him for who He is, then He is able to move in your life in ways no earthly one could ever do!

"And when the Sabbath day was come, he began to teach in the synagogue: and many hearing him were astonished, saying, From whence hath this man these things? And what wisdom is this which is given unto him, that even such mighty works are wrought by his hands? Is not this the carpenter, the son of Mary, the brother of James, and Joses, and of Juda, and Simon? And are not his sisters here with us? And they were offended at him. But Jesus said unto them, A prophet is not without honour, but in his own country, and among his own kin, and in his own house. And he could there do no mighty work, save that he laid his hands upon a few sick folk, and healed them.
- Mark 6:2-5

The word that represents *without honor* means "to despise or to hate". Can you imagine our Lord and Savior saying that the only people that hated Him were the ones in His house? It's ever so clear to a husband that comes home from work to a spouse who thinks that they're just a person that does honey-do's. In the meantime, their co-worker thinks they hung the moon. As a result, they begin to feel esteemed and valued at the job because they realized they're not honored in their own home. The Bible says that Jesus "could not" do any mighty works, not that he would not. The lack of honor stifled the flow of God coming through Jesus, the son of the living God; God in the flesh! He is Alpha and Omega, the bright and morning star, the Rose of Sharon! Yet He could not do a miracle because of the lack of honor. It says, "... Except he laid his hands upon a few sick folk and healed them." Undoubtedly, the sick folks were people who recognized the Healer in Him. In your honor will always come recognition but what you don't recognize, you cannot honor.

Have you ever had a time in your life where you had an abundant supply or somebody to help you, but because you didn't recognize it you missed your opportunity? I have. You know what that was? A lack of honor. You missed it because honor comes with recognition. When you can recognize things, you begin to see their value. There are people that I will have coffee and breakfast with. They are people that, for me, have a supply. Every time I talk to them, I get something and sometimes they don't know it. Nine times out of ten, they don't know the questions they've answered for me but because I recognize them, there's a flow that comes to me that they may be unaware of. It comes with answers, help, and with a supply. "Here goes Pastor talking about this honor stuff again. He's got clay feet like the rest of us."

Then stay where you're at, I have no problem with it. I'll tell you this much; it's a principle I learned, and it comes with the call. If you want to experience spiritual promotion, then you better understand how to be promoted. I honor my supply. Somebody went up to my spiritual father and said, "Man, he's starting to sound like you!" That's the greatest compliment I could ever be given. When I was preaching one night, a couple people said, "You sound like you have a southern accent." I'm not from the South; I'm from Philadelphia! So I'm thinking, "Where does that come from?" It comes from association and it comes by the honor in which I bestow upon my spiritual father who is from Oklahoma.

How did Jesus know they were not willing to honor Him? They were offended and offense is always present where honor is lacking. Honor is an offense buster. They were saying, "Isn't this the carpenter? Aren't his brothers sitting here with us? His sister's here. This man is going to come back here and he's going to preach to us?" But notice something, they said, "What manner of wisdom does this man have? Who is he that miracles are done by his hands?" They could recognize God, but they had a problem with the God in the man.

People justify their actions by saying, "I have my own relationship with God so I don't need anyone else." That's absolute foolishness because if you didn't need anyone else then why would Jesus give gifts unto men? People can recognize God, but not the God in the man. That is precisely why the people of Nazareth struggled with Jesus. Notice that God didn't show up and do miracles anyway, miracles just didn't happen.

Jesus did everything He did as a man anointed by God. Acts 10:38 says, "How God anointed Jesus of Nazareth with the Holy Ghost and with power who went about doing good and healing all that were oppressed of the devil." Jesus' earthly ministry was done as a man. The people of Nazareth were not blessed because they did not honor the man.

"He that receiveth you receiveth me, and he that receiveth me receiveth him that sent me. He that receiveth a prophet in the name of a prophet shall receive a prophet's reward; and he that receiveth a righteous man in the name of a righteous man shall receive a righteous man's reward.
- Matthew 10:40-41

Here is an analogy to help bring some light to a spiritual principle. As a righteous man, I might be able to give you a dollar, but in my office as a pastor, I can give you five dollars. Which one do you want? Do you want "Gene", or do you want "Pastor Gene"? I could have two different levels of reward for you. Will you still get a reward? Sure. The measure in which you receive will be the measure in which you give. They said, "Oh Jesus is just that guy, he's a carpenter!" All they seemed to be able to receive from him is a great piece of furniture. They should have recognized Jesus as Alpha and Omega, the finisher of faith, the bright and morning star, and our everything...

When you receive a wife in the office of a wife, you'll get a wife's reward. The Bible tells us that he who finds a wife finds a good thing (Proverbs 18). It doesn't say, "he who finds a woman and makes her his wife finds a good thing." That means she's supposed to be a wife when you find her, not "I can fix her! She'll change!" No, she won't. She'll change long enough to get that ring but after that, it's a wrap. The Bible says it's better to live on a corner of a roof than to live in a house with a contentious woman. Proverbs says that living with a contentious woman is like a dripping roof during a rainy day; continuous. We must recognize that if she's wife material, then she's already a wife. Likewise, she that finds a husband will find a good thing. However, if he's not working, doesn't want to work but instead wants to play video games but you're trying to turn him into a husband, move on. You don't want to find a dog. You need to find a husband, and he'll be a husband before you make him one. When you receive them in the office in which they're in, then you receive the supply that comes with that office. So if you want a good man, then you have to receive a good one.

"And we beseech you, brethren, to know them which labour among you, and are over you in the Lord, and admonish you; And to esteem them very highly in love for their work's sake. And be at peace among yourselves."
- 1 Thessalonians 5:12-13

To "know them" means "to recognize who they are." This word is the same word used when Jesus said that he knew virtue went out of him. In other words, it's not a natural understanding, I know them by the spirit"I've called my spiritual father freaking out at times and He'd say, "Alright, well thank you God." I'm thinking, "What you mean 'Thank you God?' Man I need some answers, I need some help!" Then he'd get off the phone. Eventually, I knew why he did not say anything or why he would correct me without saying anything about the situation. He was nonverbally communicating that he's about to dispatch his anointing to help solve my problem. There are situations that should have occurred in your lives, but didn't because the anointing on the church and your pastor blocked it. I watched as people who left their supply became sick, diseased, problem prone, and their life was turned upside down. One particular church may not bring the right supply for every person, but whoever they have a supply for, they are going to bless and help the congregation because that's what they are there for. There are people that will degrade me behind my back. I teach a message; they'll go home and I become their dinner. I know it by the spirit. I'll say something; they just don't like it and they'll go home and eat my lunch. You cannot partake of that behavior and still have honor. Your honor will come off disingenuous and it's easily picked up in the realm of the spirit. I know who honors me and who doesn't. I still love them and honor them, but I realize when they do not have honor. They'll have a problem with me being blessed financially. The Bible says you should not muzzle the ox and those that labor are worthy of their hire (1 Timothy 5). You do not do it for the money, but you can certainly tell if people honor you by their response when they see you prosper.

You have those friends that, as long as you're living in the same neighborhood they're living in, everybody's cool. The moment you add an upgrade to your life, they'll come to your new house with "hater" written all over their face. They'll bring accusation, "You've changed, why? You're acting new, brand new. You changed."
You're right. I changed my number; I changed my zip code and I'm changing everything else that I can!

1 Thessalonians 5 says, "Be at peace among yourself." When you honor and know those that labor among you, you have internal peace. . There were times where my life was upside down. By the time I was off the phone with my spiritual father, just hearing him say, "Well hallelujah," was enough to let me know it would be all right. It brought peace because I knew that I had help.

There is nothing like having a father in the house. The kids are more stabilized and achieve higher grades in school. Statistics shows that there's a certain peace that a child has when they have a supportive and active father.

God bless the women that have had to raise their kids by themselves. I'm not speaking ill of that at all. It's a difficult task and you should be commended for that.

It brings peace into your life when you know those that labor among you and are over you in the Lord because sometimes they're taking the hit that you should have been taking. They're more proficient and they have greater equipment to deal with the attacks. Sometimes, the attack on you is really an attack on them. People do not always understand the vigor that this work demands. It's hard to have peace within yourself when you know you're at odds with your supply. That's why people get so topsy-turvy; everything is so distressed; it's because they're not at peace. Jesus told us that everything we saw him do was because he saw His Father do it.

Whether you want to accept it or not, there is a hierarchy in the body of Christ. Jesus was submitted to God, so He walked in the power of God and He became the chief shepherd. Then, He appointed under-shepherds. When you are able to know those that are over you and when you receive them correctly. Then you'll receive the one that sent them. Familiarity always assumes too much.

The moment your leader has to correct you, be careful how you respond. Some people feel that they are "friends" with the leader, subsequently they become difficult to correct. Your Leaders are responsible for your success and your growth. Always remember that leadership is graded and judged not on the test they take, but on you passing your test. Honor and familiarity are significant problems in today's church, society, and business. We have to learn how to get that back under control.

You don't have coarse jokes with people you honor. Some people joke with me and "make fun" but you best believe I have nothing like that to say to my spiritual father, because I honor him. These are principles that are lost today and that's why the power's not there. The pastor can lay hands on you and nothing happens for you, the next person comes up with a problem they've struggled with for fifteen years and they're healed. How does that happen? How could one person come up and not be healed, but another one can? It's familiarity. "Well, I knew Pastor back when he was ...." Okay, but who he used to be can't do anything for you.

Chapter Eight:
The Art of Recognition

"He that receiveth you receiveth me, and he that receiveth me receiveth him that sent me. He that receiveth a prophet in the name of a prophet shall receive a prophet's reward; and he that receiveth a righteous man in the name of a righteous man shall receive a righteous man's reward."
- Matthew 10:40-41

How you see or receive an individual will determine what you get from that person. If you receive a person as a righteous man, then you'll get whatever that righteous man can give you. If you receive someone in the office of a prophet, then you will receive whatever the prophet can give you. When the three kings came to Elisha because they were in trouble, they were not looking for a righteous man. They had a righteous man among their midst, and it was Jehoshaphat.

"And the king of Israel said, Alas! That the Lord has called these three kings together, to deliver them into the hand of Moab! But Jehoshaphat said, Is there not here a prophet of the Lord, that we

may enquire of the Lord by him? And one of the king of Israel's servants answered and said, Here is Elisha the son of Shaphat, which poured water on the hands of Elijah."
- 2 Kings 3:10-11

In the Old Testament the only anointed offices were the prophet, priest and the king. From a New Testament perspective, we have taken on the roles of priests and kings so, therefore, the only thing left is the prophet. In the New Testament, we now have five offices in which people stand. You have the prophet, the apostle, the evangelist, the pastor and the teacher. Jehoshaphat was asking if there was anyone that he could inquire of the Lord. They felt like their lives had been delivered into the hands of their enemy by God himself. Could you imagine what it would feel like to think that God had delivered you into the hand of your enemies? A servant told them that she knew of a prophet who God was with and that he was the one who served Elijah. She recognized that the anointing that was on Elijah transferred onto Elisha. The word *anointing* means "to rub or to smear" so in other words, the way that the anointing is transferred is it's rubbed off on you. It is not taught; it's caught.

She was letting them know that Elisha walked in the office Elijah walked in and she brought confirmation by making sure he knew that he was the one that served Elijah. Elisha could have said, "I want to be known in my own right. I'm tired of being in the shadow of Elijah and everybody calling me the one who served him." He could have easily got into an egotistical position and said, "Hey listen, I'm Elisha now; Elijah is dead!" but that was not the case.

It's amazing that his servant told him and recognized the power that Elisha walked in because she told him that Elisha poured water on the hands of Elijah. Today you will not find people who are willing to stay in that level of service for any length of time. People will proclaim, "I'm anointed, I'm called, I'm tired of sweeping floors. I don't want to pour water on Pastor's hands anymore." Notice, you will find

THE ART OF RECOGNITION

nowhere in scripture does Elisha ever say he's tired of doing what he's supposed to do, and when Elijah tried to get rid of him, he said, "As the Lord liveth, I will not leave you." He understood the principle of divine relationships. She brought confirmation to the power he walked in by referencing whom he served. She didn't say, "I saw him do miracles, produce a healing, turn water into wine and lay hands on the leper."

"And Jehoshaphat said, The word of the Lord is with him. So the king of Israel and Jehoshaphat and the king of Edom went down to him. And Elisha said unto the king of Israel, What have I to do with thee? Get thee to the prophets of thy father, and to the prophets of thy mother. And the king of Israel said unto him, Nay: for the Lord hath called these three kings together, to deliver them into the hand of Moab. And Elisha said, As the Lord of hosts liveth, before whom I stand, surely, were it not that I regard the presence of Jehoshaphat the king of Judah, I would not look toward thee, nor see thee."
- 2 Kings 3:12-14

Here they have come together and they're standing before Elisha. Elisha says, "If I did not regard this man, this righteous man, I would not see any of you." Undoubtedly if he regarded Jehoshaphat's presence, then so did God. In their time of trouble, they did not need the righteous man. The three kings were already there together trying to figure out what to do. They already had a righteous man in their midst and that was not enough. They said, "Can we find someone with an anointing that we can inquire of?"

I don't need just a righteous man; I need somebody with an anointing who is a container and conduit of the power of God. Not that I can't handle it, but there are times in my life where it might seem like all hell has been released against me and what I need is the reward that comes from the prophet. Elisha needed a minstrel because the other two kings were worshiping Satan and Baal. Obviously, their prophets were not the same. Now he needs some music to get him over into his office so he can get answers. The music helped to create an atmosphere for the power of God to move. The backslidden condition of the two kings undoubtedly had an effect on the environment. That's why your leaders need you to show up in their meetings and services, bringing your supply. Just your presence, if it's in line with Christ, will help your leadership tremendously.

The problem is that, without honor, the prophet's reward cannot flow into your life because you cannot see, recognize or discern the supply that you need. They said, "Look we have a righteous man, this is not helping. We need a prophet, we need someone with an anointing, someone that can get over into the spirit realm and give us some answers." Since one man received Elisha as the prophet; a true man of God, he said, "If I didn't regard Jehoshaphat, I wouldn't see any of you." What's the difference between Jehoshaphat and the other two kings? Honor, regard and understanding. He told them, "Get to your prophets of your fathers. What you doing here?"

Honor is a distinctive problem in the church today because people want to receive you only as a righteous man; they want to receive you as a buddy, as a pal. Offense always comes when you don't discern the correct nature of the relationship because unmet expectations are always the root of offense. People that call me "Gene" don't call me "Pastor." I don't say anything, it's not my problem, but most of the time when they need me, my name changes to "Pastor Gene". Even most people who don't get it, when all hell breaks loose and they believe God has delivered them into the hands of their enemies, they come back to say,, "Wait a minute, Pastor help me." It's the worst feeling in the world. Sometimes due to their lack of honor, they have gone so far over there's little I can do. I have warned people before the trouble comes and because of a lack of honor they didn't hear it nor receive it.

THE ART OF RECOGNITION

The law of recognition is very important because when you don't recognize the prophet's reward, you operate at a lower level of supply. In other words, when I recognize the people in my life and the supply that they have, I operate at a higher degree of said supply. However, familiarity takes way too much for granted.

Familiarity will cause people to treat you differently. Now they don't care if they live up to your expectations, or if they regard what you say. They don't care if they're operating within what you've asked them to do because they've become familiar. The moment that happens, Satan begins to work on them and it's a matter of time before, if left uncorrected, they will not make it.

If you have somebody in your life and you don't recognize the supply they bring to you, you're going to lose them. I don't care if it's in a marriage, a relationship, a friendship or if it's on the job. I once heard John Maxwell say that he never worried about anyone trying to hire his assistant away from him, because he treated her with regard and he let her know how important she was to him. He further explained that if she decides she wants to go, then God bless her. However, he never struggles with that. Now, why?

He recognizes her supply. When you see it, you're not disgruntled. You only become offended when you can't discern where your help comes from anymore. If you want the reward of a wife, you've got to receive a wife. You want the reward of a husband; you've got to receive a husband. That does not mean that you agree with the individual's behavior per se, but you are constantly looking for that supply out of that person. I guarantee you, if you continue to pull on that supply, you will get it. It's just the way things pertaining to and of the spirit work. If we become carnal minded, we will only look at what we see and if we see dysfunction, we amplify dysfunction, as opposed to the Christ in the people around us.

Familiarity will try to creep into all areas of your life. If you've ever managed people, there's a delicate line between being personable without creating a relationship that will cause them to cross the line. Without warning, they show up fifteen minutes late and look at you like you've lost your mind if you dare say anything.

This is why some leaders will keep themselves somewhat insulated from certain people. I cannot trust everybody to do what they're supposed to do. The moment you place demand on them and they've gone too far with their friendship, then they have a problem with you because they're viewing your relationship as a friendship. They're trying to receive me as a righteous friend.

"Let the elders who perform the duties of their office well be considered doubly worthy of honor [and of adequate financial support], especially those who labor faithfully in preaching and teaching. For the scripture says, You shall not muzzle an ox when it is treading out the grain, and again, The laborer is worthy of their hire."
- 1 Timothy 5:17-18 AMP

My pastor, years ago, was doing cement work all day. He would come in from doing cement work in July. He, at times, would be so tanned that his skin was as dark as mine. Of course, this is from being out in the Arizona sun all day. He would then come to church and preach his heart out. I said to our leadership team at the time, "If we put in $50 a month each, our pastor can go into ministry full-time." You know what I heard? "Well brother let me pray about it," which is the Christian passive-aggressive way of saying "No."

I decided to increase my giving monthly so that he did not have to work. The art of following means that you recognize the struggles in those that you follow and because you honor them, you recognize that you want them to be blessed. Double honor would mean that if I had X amount, they're worthy of double that. Why? They're laboring in the preaching and teaching of the word and in doctrine. If it says they're worthy of adequate financial support, then it's an absolute travesty to let your man of God struggle.

I've had people in the church tell me, "Well you shouldn't get paid and you should just go get a job and do blah-blah-blah." Really? If you own the company and I walked into your company and said, "Yeah you don't deserve to be paid from this company. You should go get a job from somewhere else..." The stupidity of it all! Why do people think like that?

Why would you want your man of God to suffer? If you want the prophet's reward then you should be expecting your man of God to be at the level where he can see prosperity in his life. If he cannot get there, how will you ever get there?

It's the most insane thing I've ever heard, but it always comes from people who have no revelation. "Well, you know I just think, since you're just a servant of God you should trust God." Why do I have to trust God more than you have to trust God? I know pastors personally who have churches three times the size of Stonepoint and they're struggling because their congregation won't take care of them. How tragic is it that? A man of God, who's supposed to be giving himself to prayer and to the study of the word, has to switch hats? How tragic is it that they have to go out and start businesses? Now you have pastors that have businesses because the church will not financially support them.

See it's amazing how you see things when you really understand what the Bible's telling you. It's saying they're worthy of adequate financial support. They're worthy, doubly worthy. I truly want my spiritual father to be a multi-millionaire; multi-billionaire if he can make it there, I'm all for it! You want to know why?

I understand that nobody recognizes the things he had to give up. They don't recognize when he's sleeping in a hotel room thousands of miles away from his wife and his family and wishes he was home. While the rest of the people that he preaches to, go home and they snuggle up next to their spouses and he doesn't. Nobody understands the spiritual attack that he goes through trying to bring the level of word that he brings. Some people are always saying to me, "Pastor, the messages you're bringing and the word you're bringing is changing my life." But you have no idea the attack I have to endure to bring light to you. If I was in here just preaching, "Everything's great, we're all wonderful! You're okay; I'm okay!" We'd have little resistance. But the moment you want to open the eyes to those that are blind, you have put yourself at the front line of the attack. That's why he said those individuals are worthy of double honor. How dare you muzzle the ox! For those of you who do not understand what muzzling the ox is, let me give you a visualization.

The ox is allowed to eat while it pulls the plow because what we have learned is that the ox can only eat but so much, its one ox. Yet if you don't feed the ox, then what strength will it have to pull the plow? What are you going to do, starve the ox until he passes out? So a smart farmer says, "I'm going to allow the ox to eat," because the ox will produce way more than it eats. In the same way, the pastor must be allowed to eat. How difficult is it going to be for him to come and bring you a message when all in the back of his mind he's focused on his bills? You can get as super spiritual as you want to, call him a man of faith and power all you want, but sometimes he struggles with the same problems that everybody else has.

His supply comes from God, but it is brought through people People struggle with that concept. "I just don't know if I agree with all that." Then here's my problem, you have set yourself contrary to the word of God and I pray for you, I really do, because it's sad to watch what people do with their money..

134

A minister was on TV once talking about how his leadership team bought him a Bentley. The church became so upset that he sold it and gave the money to the children's ministry. Months later, God asked him, "Why would you do that? I moved on their hearts to bless you, to give you something for your faithfulness and commitment, and you sold it." It's amazing because if they were in his shoes, they would feel blessed to be brought something like that, but because they're not in his shoes the judgment comes. "How come he has to have that? There's starving children in Africa." Jesus said, "The poor you'll have with you always." You never judge a man because God's prospering him. He can't do anything effectively if he's not walking at the next level. I'll take this to a natural level of understanding.

There are people who want to give me financial advice all the time. "You know, Pastor if you would just do this and you would just do that and all..." they do not have fruit of financial prowess. If you want to advise me, you should demonstrate a higher level of proficiency than myself. If you want to tell me how to invest, I have no ears for you. You can say that's snobbish or conceited, but I don't deal with that and I know you don't either. Interestingly enough if we were to apply that same principle, you should expect, want and desire for those above you to prosper because it opens the door for you. You'd be shocked at how many people struggle with the prosperity of those that are in the ministry. Now do I believe that you should be wasting money while eating lobster for breakfast, lunch and dinner? No, I think you should be a wise steward of what God has given you and be able to enjoy life. You should be able to do things as your heart desires, because I cannot even describe to you in words what the pressure feels like to be in ministry. That's why he said they're worthy of double honor and adequate financial support.

In the art of following, it is imperative that we make the decision, "My man of God isn't going to struggle and he will not want for anything, plain and simple." He deserves that. I went through some serious life and ministry changes in 2012. When I told my spiritual father what I was going through and what was happening in the church. He said, "Son, I'll be there on Wednesday," hopped in his car and drove seventeen hours from Oklahoma to be here on a Wednesday evening. He didn't say, "I need money." Or, "I need a plane ticket." He didn't ask me for a thing.

That's the heart of a father. I've had people leave the church and kicked the dust off their feet when they left. Then all hell broke loose in their life (which always happens), and who do they call? Me and I start running, "What do you need? How can I help you?" First thing they say, "Pastor, I'm sorry we haven't been there." My response is, "Don't worry about it, that's not important. Here's what's important, if you need me I'm here." That's the heart that comes from someone who understands that I have a supply that people need. I do not have the right to direct my supply to where I want it to go. I have a right when people reach out to me and when they call me and say, "Pastor," I switch hats.

Anyone that has been around me when I've received those calls can see it. The office changes and I speak differently because they're pulling on the office that's in me. They're looking for the prophet's reward. When people are looking for the prophet's reward, they're dealt with differently because they are placing a demand on the office. There's always a supply because it doesn't come from me; it comes from the God who sent me. That's why Jesus said, "If you receive me, you receive him who sent me." If you don't receive the man, you can't receive what's in him and if you can't receive what's in him, I guarantee you'll start walking in offense. All it is, is a lack of honor. If you muzzle the leader, from where will they derive the strength to continue on?

Pastors are giving up and walking away from their churches at alarming rates because of hurt and disappointment. I'm not going anywhere; I'm either stupid or tenacious, I'm not quite sure which one it is yet. There are pastors that are shutting the doors and walking away because the sheep have bit them. Sheep are not carnivores; they are herbivores; they eat plants, so their teeth are flat. I think I could deal better with a dog taking a bite out of me with sharp teeth because at least he'll take a chunk and it comes out, but could you imagine a flat teeth animal just gnawing away? Why are they giving up? They're not being honored. They're paying a price and no one wants to honor them for it. I'm not talking about hero worship; we're all just human, but there's an anointing on the man for different things. If there's an anointing on man and on the word itself, then you realize that if you are in a church where the word is anointed with a leader who is anointed, then when you get revelation and clarity it is because of the flow of the anointing is there to help your life. This is why any church will not do. There's a supply for you in the place God placed you, and maybe you're saying, "I don't know if I have an anointing." It won't matter because of course you have one, but if you would come, there's an anointing on the Word that will help you. When people withdraw, things start to go south on them because they're not under the ministry of the Word. If God understood that faith comes by hearing and hearing by the word of God, then why do you think he put such a high value on those that preach and teach the word? Why do you think he says they're worthy of double honor?

If the pastor's able to do what he's called to do and feed you, everyone will be successful, prosperous and flourish. If you go to a church and find that the pastor is in a Bentley and everybody else is starving, something may be wrong. If you go to my spiritual father's church , all the people are well off. Why? He doesn't just keep it for himself, he teaches them how they can be successful. That's the way that it's supposed to be. That's the divine supply.

"Obey your leaders and submit to them, for they keep watch over your souls as those who will give an account. Let them do this

with joy and not with grief, for this would be unprofitable for you."
- Hebrews 13:17 NASB

Your spirit is sealed unto the day of redemption. Your leaders do not watch over your spirit; they watch over your soul; your mind, your will and your emotions. So why do you think there are times when they will offend your mind to reveal your heart? The job is to watch your soul. You are a spirit and if you are saved, then that is not my job. It says, "...they keep watch over your souls as those who will give an account..." You mean to tell me that we have to give an account for the way you think? Your craziness is going to be on my test? Most people are so adamant and anxious about getting into ministry, yet if they truly understood all that comes with it they would not want it. My test is graded on you, so why do you think that I will say things you don't want to hear? Why do you think I'm going to preach messages you don't want to hear?

There have been times, too often, when I'll teach on a subject that a particular person will need to hear, but they're not present to hear it.

I will ask, "Hey, you coming to church Sunday?"
"Oh no Pastor, I have to work," will be their response.

The whole reason why I'm asking is because I know by the Holy Ghost what they're struggling with and the message on Sunday will give them answers.

The Bible says, "Let them do this with joy and not with grief because that would be unprofitable for you."

Spiritual leaders are supposed to expect to lead you with joy. However, if you're causing them grief, that is unprofitable for *you;* not the leader. They have a supply for you, but if they are having a hard time dealing with you, then the only person who loses out is you.

In the church that I went to and spiritually grew up in there were only two people that started a ministry and I'm one of them. The other one was already in ministry so really there's only one person in eleven years that was actually launched out into ministry. How's that possible that out of a group of all these people that heard the same preaching, messages and were next to the same anointing that I was, how in the world is there only one person that came up out of that? It's the art of honor.

When the time came for God to give me a ministry, if I am to be honest I fought with God not to do it, but He did it anyway. Shame He don't listen to me, huh? Wish He did but, He doesn't, He's in charge. It is so easy for me to see who's most likely not to make it in ministry. You tend to be able to discern by their level of honor.

The Bible tells us to obey your leaders, not only the pastors. The leaders will have to give an account for your souls. All of you that are in leadership in some way, shape or form; you will be giving an account for those that we lead.

When you're called, nothing will scratch the itch that God has placed inside of you and, more importantly, you will be fought at the level of your call and not the level of your ignorance. That means you can deny your calling all you want to, bury yourself in a job, in school and in stuff, but if there is still a call on your life you will still be fighting at the level of your call and getting whooped at the level of your ignorance. God is not optional with his calling. Jonah got in the boat and went the other direction.

Judgment was going to come on Nineveh, so God took the prophet and said, "Go tell them to get right." God did not want to pour judgment out on Nineveh, which is why he sent the prophet. Jonah went the wrong way and said, "Let Nineveh burn." He got into the boat, went the other direction and paid the price for his own ticket. Judgment started pouring out on the boat and everybody in it. They did not do anything wrong; they just happened to be living in the same house with the one who rejected their call. The same judgment that God postponed on Nineveh is the same wrath that was released on that boat.

Sometimes the drama spread around within your family, in your house and your life is the by-product of your unwillingness to answer the call that God has placed on your life. Those on the boat didn't do anything wrong, why were they going through trouble? When they cast lots to figure out what was going overboard, Jonah came up on the short end of the stick and they threw him out of the boat. Do you ever stop to think that, in the time we're in, God needs you? As much as you want to play, ignore, and find things that are more entertaining than being at church to develop and grow into what God has called you to, did you ever stop and think that there was something that God needs you to do in this hour? Stop and think of the possibility that some of the pains you're experiencing are a direct result of your disobedience to the call. The clock is still ticking. Now what do we do about that?

This is why this book was made. You cannot lead if you can't follow; it's not possible. However, there are people that are stubborn, hard-headed, have their own way of doing things, they're going to do what they want to do and it always leads to chaos. Young people, you try to help them, but they already have all the answers. The truth of the matter is they do have all the answers but to the wrong questions. Anybody who's been on this planet for any length of time will tell you it is not about having the right answer; it's about asking the right question.

Chapter Nine:
Art of Following

Learning how to follow is very critical when you are trying to get into ministry. You have those people, the "JC and Me Crew" that are all about, "All I need is Jesus Christ and me." While you certainly only need Jesus Christ, if that was the only necessity, then why would we have so many examples of individuals in the Bible that were in divine relationships? As a matter of fact, every person in the Bible who did anything for God had a mentor. Divine relationships are necessary for your growth, and if you cannot discern your divine relationships then you're going to struggle, make mistakes and eventually get hurt.

God has sent so many to the local church to be developed, to have the bad habits dealt with and to be prepared for ministry. The moment you start to knock the edges off of them, they're gone. I don't believe that God is schizophrenic; I believe that God knows the beginning from the end. People can jump from church to church without regard for where God has placed them. Ministry is not a place that I would put someone into lightly. The Bible says, "Lay hands on no man suddenly." For those of you that like to go fisticuffs that does not mean to, "Choke somebody suddenly". The apostle Paul is saying, "Don't commission people into ministry before they're ready, lest you partake in their sin." In other words, you are responsible for those people. It is a very serious responsibility and undertaking because that which I send, I'm endorsing. One of the most sizable problems in the church is learning the art of following. People do not know how to follow. People have been taught that they don't need to be submitted to any level of authority. In their minds, submission means abuse. What if your child said to you, "I'm not going to be submitted to you as my parent because you're going to abuse me." You'd be like, "No, no I won't. I'm going to protect you." Now parents may, at times, have to beat that bootious-maximus until your cerebral cortex gets a new revelation, but they are not doing that because they hate their child or want to hurt them , they are doing it to bring correction.

My grandmother, would always say, "I'll beat you, so the cops don't have to. The difference between me and the cops? I know when to stop and they don't." When she said something, even when we grew older, we knew she slept with one eye open and her fist balled up. As we have watched generations change, they've grown a discontent for law enforcement and authority. It's a lack of respect and honor when there are video games that reward the idea of running around shooting the cops. The first time they're in a situation and they need help, who are they going to call? We have bred a society that does not respect authority, and there's an art to following. It's sad when you see those that don't know how to follow.

It is very important to bring your supply. If you work in a company, "bringing your supply" does not mean "talk on the phone all day.". I can't stand being in a store and seeing someone's talk on their cell phone while I'm waiting to get checked out. See, when people hire you; they pay you to do a job. If you don't like the pay, then don't take the job. However, if you agree to it then do the job. My grandfather would tell us all the time, "I don't care if you want to be a ditch-digger, just be the best one that you can be because that's worth respecting."

Today, people want to do as little as possible to make as much as possible and that doesn't work. It's not reciprocity. Professionally and academically, in the church, in the family and in relationships, honor is a lost art; it doesn't exist in the way that it used to. I have seen children who are 5-6 years old swearing at their parents How did we get to that place? Society knows that if you want to steal the power of something, you remove the honor of it. If you can steal the honor, you will steal the power. You want to take the power out of a marriage, a family or a church? Take the honor out of it.

According to one Gallup Pole, 1,500 pastors in the United States are quitting the ministry every single month. Do you want to know why they're walking away? They're frustrated because there's no honor. According to the same pole, many churches are opening every single year and almost twice as many are shutting down. Why would they just walk away from the call of God completely? Anytime you have hurt and offense, you will tend to find an absence of honor.

People get offended with the ministry, the pastor, their brothers and sisters, and it is always because of a lack of honor. You cannot be offended at that which you honor because when you honor, you give more credit. You start to look at a person in light of what their intentions might have been versus their actions. As people, we judge ourselves in light of our intentions but we judge everyone else based on their actions. When the actions and their intentions don't line up, if it's in our favor then we are okay with it but when it's not in our favor, then we pickup offense. Instead of just saying that this could have been a mistake. When you honor, you'll come and request clarification before you overreact Honor is an understanding that you're submitted and you're not equals.

Familiarity always assumes undue intimacy. I don't approach anybody as if I'm on the same level even if I think I am. I automatically render honor into whom honor is due. If they've been in the ministry longer than I have. If they have an equal anointing or

THE ART OF FOLLOWING

higher they get double honor from me. Not that I disregard or disrespect people who are not, I give them honor too because you owe everybody respect, but if they're over me, they get double honor. Those are the ones that are able to speak into my life.

When Miriam and Aaron tried to discuss Moses dating the Ethiopian woman, God called them outside to speak with them. He proceeded to tell them that He spoke to them in visions and dreams but to Moses he spoke mouth to mouth. In other words, to them He spoke vaguely giving them types and shadows and bits and pieces. But unto Moses, he spoke to him face to face. The Bible says that the children of Israel knew the acts of God, but Moses knew the ways of God. It's one thing to know a person's behavior, but it's another to know why they do it. When you understand rank and authority, you don't have a problem with recognizing it. When God brought correction to Moses, he used Jethro, Moses' father in law. Why? He's older, more experienced and Moses had already submitted to him. That's how correction comes.

You get people that come into the church thinking they can tell the pastor how to do everything. First of all, they don't know why everything is done the way it is. Maybe the church secretary can't type worth a lick, but maybe she's more faithful than all of you. There might be people that couldn't handle being fired or stepped down and you're wondering, "Why are we doing it this way?" It's not your place to wonder why; it's your place to do.

Recognizing the authority in those that are over you and those that you have selected to submit yourself to is of the utmost importance. If you go to a church and the pastor is not submitted to somebody, you should run.

"I'm an apostle."

First thing I say is, "Who's your pastor?"

"I'm an apostle, so I don't need one."

The devil is a liar!

You must be accountable to somebody because if you can't follow the man you can see, you can't follow the one you can see. Accountability is a very, very important aspect of following, but yet and still you will find that most people struggle with that.

Ephesians tell us that you are supplied by the supply in which you bring. Every joint has a supply, so when you have a responsibility in the local church or in ministry, when you bring your supply to that you receive one. If you refuse to bring your supply, or if you bring it in a dysfunctional way, then your supply is diseased. If my wrist started to shut down on me, my hand is going next because the supply that goes to my hands goes through my wrist. When the wrist does its job, it receives a supply and then it comes through the wrist to whatever's connected to it. So when you are in ministry, you bring your supply by being positioned in the joint where you're supposed to be. So if you are the knee, then be the knee. If you are the armpit, God forbid, then you're the armpit. The Bible says that more grace is given to the less comely parts.

When you don't bring your supply, you're stuck. You're sitting there warming the pew, warming the chair, but you won't bring a supply. You wonder why all these other people are striving as hard as they are in the ministry; they are contending for the faith. It's because they've come to the understanding that if they seek His kingdom and His righteousness then all the other things will be added. But if I will not bring my supply in a way that is conducive to what I was designed to bring my supply to, then I have no right to receive a supply.

The reason why you honor and esteem those above you highly is because of the work that they do. It's no easy task to serve God. You render honor unto those who serve God because they're among the elite few that have decided that they're going to take the hits, kicks,

145

THE ART OF FOLLOWING

punches that comes with serving God in a world that is anti-God. They deserve honor just because they made the decision to serve Him and any decision to serve God will always put you completely against Satan. If you're never running into Satan, if you're never bumping heads with him, then you are both headed in the same direction.

You have to find a place where you say, "I'm going to esteem them because they're doing the job for the work's sake!" If nothing else, it's for the work's sake. He said, "Be at peace among yourselves and to know those that labor among you." The word "know" is the same Greek root word as "perceive", meaning "know those that labor among you." When the woman with the issue of blood came in and she touched the hem of Jesus' garment, Jesus said, "I perceive that somebody touched me." In other words, to discern them— not after the flesh, the Bible says we know no man after the flesh—by the spirit. That's a difficult thing, because what if the flesh is ticking you off? What if their flesh is about as rough as sandpaper? What if their flesh is just really rubbing you the wrong way?

Let me tell you something, if you don't discern who your spouse is, you'll miss it and they'll know you missed it. It will not end up well. Why do people step out of their relationships? They find that there's some supply they're not receiving. You can say what you want to say, I've done a lot of marriage counseling over the years and I can tell you this much; nobody that I've counseled that has been through a spouse stepping out on them left for no reason. They may not have said the reason at the time, but in counseling the reason always comes to the surface. What is it?

There's zero discernment of their supply. At some point in time, you begin to look at each other with familiarity. For one reason or another she's not the jewel she once was. Now all of a sudden, he's not the guy who hung the moon like he used to.

The saddest thing in the world is for you to not recognize where your supply is. We have people that drive over an hour each way to come to our church. If you don't know, if you don't recognize it, you'll miss it and you'll miss out on opportunity, growth, blessing and you won't be at peace.

Have you ever been in a place and you just don't like the environment. The hairs on the back of your neck are standing up, you have a bad feeling and you want to leave. You're not at peace with yourself are you? There's a point where you find the place that makes the baby in your belly leap, the place where you come by the spirit.

In their respective wombs, Jesus and John the Baptist were not able to talk to each other. John's in Elizabeth, Jesus is in Mary, but yet and still when they greeted each other there was something in the realm of the spirit that John recognized. He leaped, and when he did he was filled with the Holy Ghost. I'm not talking about recognizing people naturally; I'm talking about discerning your supply spiritually. You cannot follow if you don't know where your supply is. You cannot follow if that baby in your belly's not leaping. There's a peace that comes when you know that you're finally in the place where you belong.

If the Lord told me to give my watch to a specific person, but I give it to someone else, can I apply any faith to that? What if I said, "You know, I kind of like my watch, so here's what I'm going to do. I'm going to give them this pen. I've grown accustomed to my watch and this thing cost 50,000 times more than this one. So I'll just give them that. I can't apply faith to that. In the same way, if God placed you in the body where He decided, then if God put you in a particular church and you decide, " I'm going to go somewhere else," you can't apply faith to that. You certainly can do it as people do it all the time.

That's why he said "...be at peace among yourselves..." Because peace comes when you know where you are and you understand your supply. Statistical studies show that kids that have both their mother and their father are more settled than those that have single parents. Not that single parents are bad; situations are what they are, but when you're settled, you have greater peace.

There are some people I've preached out the door. I know they're wolves , I know exactly what they're struggling with and when they hear what they don't want to hear they'll leave. It's the word of God, but they'll get very tired of hearing it and then they're gone. Sometimes I will have to deal directly with the wolves. The goats and the sheep, they all stay and then I deal with them the same. God will separate the goats and the sheep at the end and I'm so glad that's His job. My job is to watch out for the wolves. In the natural, goats and sheep can co-habitate. There have been stories that they can even feed each others young. As for the wolves, they have to go!

There are people that should have left our church over the years and I'm absolutely fine with it. However, there are people that should be here and the moment they left, they lost their peace. I've seen them lose their healing, they get sick as a dog, and you have to ask yourself, Is it really worth it? I'd rather be where my supply is, receive it and follow because if I follow, recognize and esteem them highly in love for the work's sake, then the Bible says I get to be at peace.

Some time ago we had a guy at our church. For the protection of the innocent, we will change his name to Skippy. Skippy had not been going to our church for more than a week, maybe two, and had the audacity to ask me, "So who preaches when you're not here?" Not Skippy! Zealous, but unskilled and didn't know how to follow. Skippy could drop the name of every pastor in town and to my knowledge, Skippy is still sitting at home being the greatest prophet that ever lived. He always has a word for somebody, what I call prophe-lie.

Anyone can prophesy but when prophecy contains revelation, then 1st Corinthians 14 tells us that it needs to be judged. This does not mean parking lot prophecy. There is always that person that has a word for you in the parking lot. There are a lot of people that have the prophetic gifts in their life, but they're not being done in decency and in order.

People will say, "I love the gifts of the spirit!" But they don't know anything about them so, they flow in a way that causes harm. Remember the Bible says if everybody's praying in tongues and the unlearned walk in, they're going to think everybody's mad. You walk into some churches, boy as soon as the music hits, people take off running, rolling on the floor, screaming and hollering in tongues; no decency and no order. Then you've got the extreme opposite of that where the spirit of God is not allowed to move in the service when it's His church.

"And he came to the sheepcotes by the way, where was a cave; and Saul went in to cover his feet: and David and his men remained in the sides of the cave. And the men of David said unto him, Behold the day of which the Lord said unto thee, Behold, I will deliver thine enemy into thine hand, that thou mayest do to him as it shall seem good unto thee. Then David arose, and cut off the skirt of Saul's robe privily. And it came to pass afterward, that David's heart smote him, because he had cut off Saul's skirt. And he said unto his men, The Lord forbid that I should do this thing unto my master, the Lord's anointed, to stretch forth mine hand against him, seeing he is the anointed of the Lord. So David stayed his servants with these words, and suffered them not to rise against Saul. But Saul rose up out of the cave, and went on his way."
- 1 Samuel 24:3-7

David ran up behind Saul and asked why was Saul chasing him. He compared himself to a dog and a flea. Why would David have the opportunity in the cave to kill Saul and not take it? For those of you that may not know what cover his feet means, it meant that Saul went in there to relieve himself. So Saul is in a very compromising position. God told David that he would deliver Saul into his hands and that David can do with him what he saw fit. God didn't tell him to kill or attack him, He let David decide. David and Saul had a very tumultuous relationship. David was revered by the people because he had the anointing. He represented God's choice and Saul represented man's choice.

Be careful of people in your life that have a Saul spirit on them. They don't want you to do what they couldn't do. Some of you have family members that were supposed to be in ministry and now because they were burnt by it, they talk garbage to you. They don't want you to do what they were supposed to do or do it any better than they did it because excellence always brings agitation to those who are not excellent.

You go up in the job and start doing the best job possible. Clean the floors until they sparkle, so the boss comes in and slides from one end to the other. Everybody will start talking about you because you're excellent. In the church, unfortunately among our own people, if somebody starts doing excellence, people start, "Who do they think they are?" Excellence rubs people the wrong way because when one operates in excellence it forces the other one to be circumspect about their mediocrity.

David was anointed; he was anointed and chosen by God. Saul accepted him when he was delivering the kingdom from the Philistines, but all of a sudden Saul started getting agitated with David because he started to be seen as God's choice. Now Saul's trying to kill him and David and his men are hiding.

David was anointed to be king; he was the next in line. If it was anybody's kingdom, it belonged to David. All he had to do was come in, kill Saul and it's his, but David cut off the hem of his skirt and that bothered him. It smote his heart because he said, "I can't touch God's anointed. I want to, but I can't. I sure would love to, but I won't." And he ran after Saul saying, "I am but a dead dog, a flea. Why are you chasing after me?" He had God on his side because he was chosen, but yet and still he refused to put his hands on the one that God delivered to him.

God didn't say, "Kill him," because if God told David to kill him, he would have. He had enough regard to say, "I can't do this; God chose him. If God is the one that sets up kings and tears down kings, then God will have to deal with him. If He chooses to be merciful or to pour judgment, praise the Lord, but it is not my job." Saul is in there relieving himself, yet and still, David had enough honor to say, "No, I can't do this."

There are pastors and preachers that have Saul spirits and God will deal with them. The Bible says it repented God that he ever made Saul king and although He was disappointed in Saul, He never fired him. God could have killed him, but you mean to tell me our God has a regret of something that happened as if He couldn't do anything about it? The Bible says that "… the gifts and callings are without repentance." God will not give it and take it away. When God gives you an anointing, He will not take it back from you. I don't care what you've been through, what you've done or what mistakes you've made, the gifts and callings of God are without repentance. He will never take it back. That's why He won't give it to you easily. Once He gives it to you, He can't take it back and He expects you to walk it out. If you fall off the track then you get back up again and become skillful.

"And David said unto the young man that told him, How knowest thou that Saul and Jonathan his son be dead? And the young man that told him said, As I happened by chance upon mount Gilboa, behold, Saul leaned upon his spear; and lo, the chariots and horsemen followed hard after him. And when he looked behind him, he saw me, and called unto me. And I answered, Here am I. And he said unto me, Who art thou? And I answered him, I am an Amalekite. He said unto me again, Stand I pray thee, upon me, and slay me; for anguish is come upon me, because my life is yet whole in me. So I stood upon him, and slew him, because I was sure that he could not live after that he was fallen: and I took the crown that was upon his head, and the bracelet that was on his arm, and have brought them hither unto my Lord. Then David took hold of his clothes, and rent them; and likewise all the men that were with him..."
- 2 Samuel 1: 5-11

"And David said unto him, How wast thou not afraid to stretch forth thine hand to destroy the Lord's anointed? And David called one of the young men, and said, Go near, and fall upon him. And he smote him that he died.
- 2 Samuel 1:14-15

This guy saw that Saul was dying and Saul asked him to put him out of his misery. The young man did so, following orders and then brought his bracelet and ring to David. David responded to the overwhelming gesture of loyalty, "How was it that you were not afraid to touch God's anointed?" David ordered for the young man to be killed.

That question is very thought provoking. If somebody brought me the crown and said, "I took this from him and brought it to you, my lord," one would think that I would be ecstatic and appreciative. But if

I was king and realized this man had no fear of killing the king, then I could eventually be in danger.

My mom would tell me this; "If a dog brings a bone, he'll carry one." If they come to you trying to slay somebody, they will slay you, as well. Here this man is bringing him the crown and you would think that it was a measure of honor, but the first thing David said was, "How in the world were you not afraid? This was God's anointed. You mean to tell me there wasn't an ounce of fear in you?"

Be very cautious of people that have no fear of the work of God. After I was licensed sent from my church, I never called one person in that church. If they called me I did not take the phone call. I did not want the people to think I was attempting to damage another man's church. I'll leave peaceably first. Woe be unto the person who has no fear of God. I've watched people split a church right down the middle, take sides against the pastor and rally the troops. David said, "This guy has to die because he's not afraid." A man who's not afraid of anything is a dangerous person.

Saul was dying anyway he just made sure he was dead. Saul couldn't live from that kind of wound so he was helping Saul out. He just happened to be in the area. You have to ask yourself, did God allow him to be in that area? Did God use him to deliver the crown? Did God use him to do what David would not do? David's now king, Jonathan's dead, Saul is dead, but the only question was, "How come you are not afraid to touch God's anointed?

King Saul was crazy as a loon. David had honor for the Lord's anointing because he was about to be in the same office. The same regard of how you deal with your leaders will be the same regard of what you'll receive when you're in that office. Be not deceived God is not mocked. Which is why when I sowed, I sowed into my future. When I gave to and served my pastor, I sowed into my future. I knew that God had a call on my life and I knew that whatever I planted I was going to reap. If I wanted to have people who were loyal and committed, then I was going to be loyal and committed so when the time came, God would bring me people that would regard, respect and honor in the same way that I honored the man of God that He put me with.

There's more at risk than your feelings. Some of you that serve in the ministry, I hope when the day comes you have people that serve like you do. For some, that's excitement and for others it's an indictment. It's sad, but it's true. Honor will cause you to see things from a very different perspective.

"There came unto him a woman having an alabaster box of very precious ointment, and poured it on his head, and he sat at meat. But when his disciples saw it, they had indignation, saying, To what purpose is this waste? For this ointment might have been sold for much, and given to the poor. When Jesus understood it, he said unto them, Why trouble ye the woman? For she hath wrought a good work upon me. For ye have the poor always with you; but me ye have not always. For in that she hath poured this ointment on my body, she did it for my burial. Verily I say unto you, Wheresoever this gospel shall be preached in the whole world, there shall also this, that this woman hath done, be told for a memorial of her. The one of the twelve, called Judas Iscariot, went unto the chief priests, and said unto them, What will ye give me, and I will deliver him unto you? And they covenanted with him for thirty pieces of silver."
- Matthew 26: 7-15

Judas was the one who questioned why Mary would put the oil on Jesus' feet and then the disciples began to talk that way. They're wondering, "Why was this wasted?" The Bible goes on to tell us that Judas was not concerned about the money for the poor, but he was the treasurer and so he was looking for the money for himself. Immediately thereafter, it says that Satan entered into his heart to betray Jesus. As Jesus was sitting at the table, they're asking him, "Hey which one's going to get to sit next to you? Who's the one who's going to be next to you when we get to heaven?" They're all plotting on their position next to Jesus, and Jesus begins to tell them about how one of them is going to betray him. Then, they all are going around the table wondering, "Is it I, Lord? Is it me? Who's it going to be?"

Jesus had spiritual discernment because he did not hear it naturally; they were murmuring about it. The Bible says when Jesus *understood* this, not when he *heard* it. He never heard it; he perceived it by the spirit. He explained that Mary was preparing him for his burial. In other words, what she's doing is of God, but think of where your heart, mind and your revelation would have to be to stand up with indignation against the son of God, our God in the flesh, and question Him as to what He's doing. The one who lead this revolt is the one who ended up betraying him.

You have to listen and believe Satan for those thoughts to enter into your heart and start to work on you. They were all thinking it; all of them were indignant, but it's not about what you think, it's about how it affects what you say and do. The undoing of Christ might have been necessary at some point in time to come, but woe be unto the man through which it comes. You have to ask, "Did God use Judas for this purpose?" Jesus picked him. He knew he was going to be betrayed, but still picked him. Yet and still because of his heart, Judas could not submit to Christ, he couldn't follow. The rest of the guys followed. That does not mean they did not have questions, concerns or disagreed with certain situations but the difference is they remained faithful to God but Judas did not. What makes a Judas?

Judas had the ability to go to the Roman guards against Christ and yet sit at the table with Christ. Be careful of people in your life that can cross both sides. They can be for you one minute and then they can go fraternize with people who don't like you the next.

Familiarity will cause you to think that you have a voice. You don't have a voice; you have a position and a function. Your voice is earned through commitment. You stick through the tough times and when all hell breaks loose and you're still shoulder to shoulder with me, that's when you earn a voice. Until then, you don't have one. It would help you if you choose your friends that way. Don't let the girls who don't have a man tell you how to deal with yours. They have to earn a voice. How do they earn a voice? They demonstrate proficiency by being with you when all hell breaks loose in your life. They're not there to watch you go down, but to help you up. Some people will stick around just to watch you fall. We can't be afraid to look for their fruit. The world will say you are judging and they're right. There are things I am able to judge. I'm able to judge your fruit; that's how I tell what type of tree you are. We get into this no-judging thing and all of a sudden we just lay down for anything. "Everything's okay, everything's fine. We'll just accept it because we're Christians; we're everybody's doormat." I don't know where that came from but I am not anyone's doormat.

Chapter Ten:
The Art of Excellence

Excellence means to be preeminent, to be outstanding and to surpass. Let's be honest, today you don't find anything that surpasses your expectations anymore. For example, the quality of service that you get when you go out to dinner is horrendous. Very rarely do you ever find anything that surpasses your expectations. I used to think that it had a lot to do with how much money you spent. I figure if you're in better restaurants, and you spend a lot more money, you would end up getting better service. To be honest with you, that is simply not true. In today's society, excellence is a lost art form.

You ever heard the term, "Go the extra mile?" Jesus said for us to go the extra mile. Roman soldiers in those times could bring their bags and their gear to your house for help. If they came to your home, you were obligated to carry their bag for them one mile. This is how they moved infantry, rations and supplies. Jesus said, "If you carry it one mile, carry it another one," just to show the type of person that you are.

If "excellent" means "to be preeminent," then that means you take a certain level of care about who you are as a person and you recognize that whatever you do, you are autographing with your signature. However, you handle assigned tasks, your school work, your job, your family or your children and even how you treat your possessions is a reflection of your level of excellence. Think about the word "preeminent." Jesus said, "Go the extra mile." If you're a Christian, you are head and shoulders are above the rest. It's amazing how people want to be the head and not the tail, but they act more like the tail than they do the head.

It says to excel above the rest. That means you're different;you're not the same as everybody else. It's funny when you go into a job or workplace; you are called the boss' pet if you try to excel at your job. Where did the shift happen that we made the decision that we don't have to do the best that we can?

I cannot imagine having to go through what our Lord and Savior went through. You had to have an excellent spirit; you had to be able to see the vision and know that the future would be greater than your present. Your future has to be seen as greater than the discomfort of your present. People today don't want to be excellent and don't see the need to be either.

I was a good, solid C student. I'd get a B every once in awhile, maybe even an A on occasion, but I was a solid C. To be real honest with you I was absolutely bored in school. So for me, all I did was enough to get by. That wasn't good enough and I regret it. Often times I see that type of mentality reflected in areas of people's lives, but mediocrity is not the pinnacle of success. No one has been successful being mediocre, being average, being par, or on the middle of the line.

"Then this Daniel was preferred above the presidents and princes, because an excellent spirit was in him; and the king thought to set him over the whole realm."
- Daniel 6:3

158

The people and the princes around him and those that served with him, they sought to find where Daniel was making mistakes and interestingly enough they couldn't find any. So they resorted to trickery, to get the king to decree it so that Daniel would be an infractor. Haters and people who are against you in life, if they cannot find occasion against you for real reasons, often times they will fabricate what they need in order to serve their goals and bring occasion against you.

Daniel was a man who lived his life in such a way that even those that were looking to find occasion against him couldn't. He operated with such excellence; I don't mean perfection, I mean excellence. There's a difference; perfection is where you hold yourself to a standard that you can't do. Excellence is when you do the best you can with what you have. If you're a two talent person, then you do what you can do with your two talents. If you're a five talent person, you do what you can do with your five talents. God does not expect you to do more than what you are capable of, He expects you to use what you have.

Excellence does not have excuses. We have a responsibility to people. To serve them and to provide an atmosphere that is conducive to their growth and success as a church. We have a job function that has been mandated by God and divinely orchestrated by him. How in the world can we come up with an excuse? If this is the bar, set the bar where it should be and hit the mark. Excellence is when you go above and beyond and say, "You know what? I'm preeminent; I'm outstanding. In God, I can do all things. I'm honorable towards what God has called me to do."

It's amazing and it's not just in the congregation, it's even in the ministry leaders and the Five Fold Ministry, those that know better but yet they're lazy about their ministry. You can always spot people that have a high level of faith. When you put them in ministry, you can tell because the first thing they want to know is how can we make this the best it can possibly be. An average thinker wants to know what do we need to get by right now.

I'm not interested in fixing the problem that we have right now; I'm interested in fixing the problem we're going to have in five-ten years. If we are preeminent then, we are people of excellence who hold ourselves to a different standard so when people try to seek occasion against us, they can't. Some people, you don't even have to seek an occasion. They're so sloppy an occasion against them comes to you.

The Bible says Daniel handled himself so well that the king suffered no harm. The king never took a hit because Daniel was on the scene. That's where someone can leave you in charge and know that it'll get handled just as if they were sitting there, not as if it's an opportunity to shine and do things their own way. They'll think that since the leader is away that he will never know. Excellence is when you carry yourself to a whole different standard. The king knew that if he put Daniel in charge, he would suffer no damage. People wouldn't complain about him. He wouldn't leave projects undone. The king did not have to put his mind on it.

Could you imagine if our President had to worry about who's going to mow the lawn? I don't want that man worrying about who's going to mow the lawn or who's going to clean the guns. What I want him to do is focus on fixing this country, that's his job. Yet and still what we don't understand is that when you are in a corporation, a business, a church, or wherever it is; if the lawn doesn't get mowed, somebody has to be responsible for it. If the floors don't get swept, somebody has to be responsible for it. If the church doesn't get setup, somebody has to be responsible for it. The moment that you have to go there in your head to deal with those items, you have just been derailed from the true focus of the job.

What if we were talking about a CEO? You have to recognize that the responsibility of the vision lies on the leader, but he cannot do that if people are not excellent at what they do. Mediocrity will always affect an organization. You can always determine what's mediocre; it's average. How do you know what is not average? People are wowed! "Wow" goes above average, "wow" invokes a spirit of excellence. It's preeminent and outstanding! The Bible says the reason why Daniel had these characteristics is because he had an excellent spirit within him. Not an excellent soul, not an excellent mind, not an excellent body. He was not the most handsome and the most dashing. He had an excellent spirit. See when you understand and recognize that, then you can ask yourself if you have an excellent spirit. Well, I want to ask you a question. If you have the Holy Spirit who lives on the inside of you then I would hope you would recognize and discern that you do have an excellent spirit. But why do we not understand that if the Holy Ghost teaches us all things, if the Holy Ghost is the one that brings all things to remembrance in the scripture, then why do we struggle with excellence? Our flesh and our soul try to take over everything we do. If I were to sit down and talk to somebody going into ministry, I would tell them to be excellent. Be the one that Pastor can trust. Be that one that will do it the way you are asked to and not the way you feel the bar should be lowered. It amazes me how when I set the bar higher, people constantly want to come and say, "Yeah but can we do this?" No, in your house you do it the way you want to. In this house we are, in my opinion, preeminent. We are Christ-like; so everyone in this organization is going to hold the bar of excellence because that's what we do, that's who we are. People always tell me that I am radical. Beautiful, keep it moving and don't hurt the rest of us. As long as there is oxygen in my body, I expect excellence, and I would not expect it from you if I did not do it myself. I bring everything I have to what I do because that's who I am. Solving problems is what I do. I don't talk about problems, I don't report the problem, I solve it. What about you, are you a problem solver? Are you a paycheck taker or a difference maker.

The spirit of excellence is not in everybody. Let me tell you something, if you are working in a company and you're one of the leaders, you better watch people under you because you can always tell who has an excellence spirit and who doesn't. The ones who don't hang by the water cooler talking and need 50 million smoke breaks. The people of excellence are the ones that will be there. They arrive early and they leave late. They're not complaining about what time they need to be somewhere.

I have ran several companies over my career and it never ceases to amaze me how people will run out of the building at 5 o'clock. Now it stands to reason that it at least takes you a couple minutes to get your stuff together, so how you leave at 5:00 P.M. on the dot. I do not know. To me, you just robbed me of a few minutes of work. They run out the door like the school bell rang. The same thing happens in church. Service is released and people are out the door like somebody shot off a gun. Where's the excellence? You might be done with your work but how can you help someone else with theirs? How can we make this a little bit better? Maybe the floor got swept, but it'd look nicer if we mopped it. How do we take it to the next level?

Don't get into ministry if you're not going to be excellent. You want to know why? Satan will eat your lunch if you're not paying attention to the details. I have a saying, "There are no trolls." You know how in fiction stories at night, everybody goes to sleep and then the trolls come out and they do all the stuff, fix and build everything, then when you wake up it's all done! I don't have trolls, plain and simple. So if I go to bed and it wasn't done, I'm going to wake up and it still won't be done. We have a responsibility to understand that if we are excellent, then there's no occasion that can be found against you.

People will take the victimized position and ask why are they being "picked" on. You're sloppy. Let's call it what it is. Love you, but you're sloppy. That's why you get "picked" on all the time. Because see, Daniel did not say, "Why is everybody picking on me..." Because they could not. He operated and carried himself so that they had to create a problem to hold against him because they could not find one. Everything you do, the Bible tells you to do it as unto God. Do we even realize that everything we do for God, every position in the church, every job you work at, God is looking at you going, "Do this as if you're doing it unto me?" How can you be a witness to other people if you are sloppy? If you act like they act, how are you going to tell them that there's a God that will empower you to be successful if you can't do it?

An excellent spirit will surpass expectations. Have you ever heard the saying that you don't get what you expect, you get what you inspect? When you inspect, then they know there's pressure that someone is looking over their shoulders. But it always amazes me how people do not come to the realization that God is the chief inspector. He can discern the intentions of your heart. Knowing that God is the ultimate fruit inspector, to some of you that's an indictment and to others it's encouragement. God can discern the very nature of your heart. Daniel was preferred above everyone else; above all the presidents and princes because there was an excellent spirit in him.

People will sometimes say that you have to be fair and everybody needs to be treated the same? You know that's a lie, don't you? God is not fair; God is just. There's a difference. In the Parable of the talents the Bible says that to one God gave five, to one He gave ten, to another He gave one. God is not fair; He's just. He divides unto whomever He desires based on their abilities. They had different capacities. It's not fair; it's equitable. An excellent spirit sets you apart from others. Daniel was preferred because he was excellent; he was preferred because he was different; he was a man of integrity and got the job done. The king wasn't running around behind him asking if he collected taxes today. Did you get this today? Hey, did you do that? The king never had to touch it, which made him excellent.

There's a process that everybody goes through when they come to the church and it's the same for every person. When they speak about the church, they will say, "Pastor, I really like coming to your church." Then, at some point they will begin to start saying, "Pastor, I really love our church." Finally, they're saying, "Pastor, I love my church." What happens is people start taking true ownership of that which really does not belong to me, it belongs to the body of Christ. The church is not here for me; it's here to develop you, teach you, train you, and prepare you to become fully developed followers of Christ.
You may walk into someone else's house, you might say, "Well it's not as clean as I'd like it to be, but you know it's not my house." But when you go into your house, all of a sudden you begin to see things a little differently because it's your house. But vision can be a very, very dangerous thing. You want to know why? The easiest way to steal a person's vision is to give them another one.

"At midday, O king, I saw in the way a light from heaven, above the brightness of the sun, shining round about me and them which journeyed with me. And when we were all fallen to the earth, I heard a voice speaking unto me, and saying in the Hebrew tongue, Saul, Saul, why persecutest thou me? It is hard for thee to kick against the pricks. And I said, Who art thou, Lord? And he said, I am Jesus whom thou persecutest. But rise, and stand upon thy feet; for I have appeared unto thee for this purpose, to make thee a minister and a witness both of these things which thou hast seen, and of those things in the which I will appear unto thee..."
- Acts 26: 13-16

Paul, standing before King Agrippa, was not disobedient to the heavenly vision. In chains, he was not ashamed because of the bondage. He'd been bonded since the moment he received the vision. The vision that he received was that he was going to testify what he had seen and what God was going to show him. Notice, when he had his Damascus experience, he said, "Is that you, Lord?" He was blinded on the road to Damascus. Now why was he blinded? God was giving him another vision, so He took his natural eyesight away from him. Your eyesight will always lead to your insight, but they are not one in the same. You can have eyesight and no insight and vice versa. God was giving him a new vision along with instruction of what to do. We then see in Paul's life a dedication to the vision. The Bible says in Proverbs 29 that literally the people perish without a vision. If you read it in the NIV, it says they cast off restraint when they have no redemptive revelation. You know what a redemptive revelation of God is?

Let me help you to get a picture of a redemptive revelation. You all, at one point in time prior to Christ, have put yourself in compromising positions that you were not supposed to be in. Some of you went to the club with a bottle full of whatever. Some of you were dancing it up, some of you "every day you was shuffling." Then there came a point where you recognized your redemption in Christ. You became clearer about what God expects from you and of who God is and what He is in your life. So, you lived your life a certain way and then you came to the realization, Hey wait a minute, God expects more. Then you begin to realize there's more to this than that. The decision is made that you're not going to stay in this low-level place of thinking. You began to get a redemptive revelation of who you are, which means that your understanding of who you are is now viewed through your redemption. Who you are is now viewed in the light of your redemption it is not who you used to be. I don't care if you think you are the most sanctified, holy-rolling person that ever walked the planet. Who you are today is nothing compared to what you look like through the lens of God's redemptive plan and purpose for you.

God's vision always comes through a redemptive revelation. In other words, it comes from His perspective, not yours. He is seeing it through the lens of what you're supposed to be and not what you currently are. This is a unique challenge for a pastor, because when the pastor begins to deal with his flock, he is not speaking to who you are in the flesh. He is speaking to who you are in the spirit. The office of the pastor gives a unique God inspired perspective.

You can have knowledge, but not have a redemptive understanding. You have to ask yourself, is your church, reaching the full redemptive potential that God has for it? Is it really at the place where God wants it to be? Not, "Is it good enough for me? Does it take care of my needs and my family?" We have to realize that there is a redemptive plan and that plan is always seen in light of the redemption that's been offered to you. Christ did not die for you to live an average life. John 10:10 tells us that Jesus came that we might have an abundant supply, more than enough, to the full, until it overflows. There's one thing to do something great; it's another to put your life on the line. He did not do all of that for you to be average.

There's an old joke where the cow and the pig and the chicken got together and they said, "You know, farmer has been real nice to us. He's fed us and taken care of us. I think we should do something nice for him. Maybe we should make him breakfast." The pig looked at the cow and the chicken and said, "That's easy for you, but for me to supply the bacon I've got to give up my life."

It is literally a slap in the face for you not to recognize that Christ laid his life down for you to be redeemed, to be pulled out of the world. It's a shame to go back to low-level living and not realize that the redemption that draws nigh unto you was brought into your life for you to be preeminent and outstanding. People should look at you and go, Wow! I hate them. They always show up early; they're always staying late. Of course, the last thing they will be saying is that they can't believe you are their boss. Your redemption made you excellent. A cut above the rest!

The sign of the anointing is I can do more with less. If I need to work twice as hard to get half as much, I'm operating under a curse and it's time for me to check some things and get myself in order. Might be the way I think, the way I feel or the things I'm doing, but if I have to do more to get less, what do I need God for? The sign that God's favor is upon my life is that I'm able to do more with less. When you're able to do more with less, trust me when I tell you that you will invoke a green spirit in most people. They will get jealous. Now, your Christian brothers and sisters, they won't get jealous because they're holy and they recognize that the same spirit that dwells in you dwells in them. All they'll have to do is get up and go be excellent too, right? If only that were true. Some of your worst critics will come from inside the church. Some of your worst sabotage will come from your Christian brothers and sisters who will be smiling in your face, all the while they want to take your place. But a redemptive revelation does not allow you to see it any more than the way God wants it to be. Not with your resources, but with His. Not with your vision but with His. Not with your ability but with His! God said His ways are higher than your ways; His thoughts are higher than your thoughts. You could think ahead to your fastest moment and God will be sitting there waiting for you when you get there. Paul was given a vision and the vision was to do what God had revealed to him. Now here's the thing, Paul said that by all measures of education that he was a Pharisee. He was as smart if not smarter than the rest of them. Do you realize that Paul was already excellent? All he needed was a direction, a vision. When people don't have a vision, they cast off restraint, they have no order anymore; they perish. They can't see it anymore and they have no guidelines by which to live. Listen, You should not be excellent because someone is watching or supervising. Be excellent because that's who you are. People that aren't excellent hate being supervised.

They don't want to be "micromanaged." Do your job with excellence and you won't be.

The Apostle Paul left Timothy at Ephesus. Timothy was fairly young. We know this because Paul wrote him a letter telling him to not let anyone despise his youth. When Paul was writing about Timothy, he commented that there was a gift in him. That it was in his grandmother and mother. When I read that, I began to think to myself, "Why would he have stated where it came from?" Obviously, that is where it comes from. If we are lacking of excellence, sometimes we have to look at how we were reared.

My parents did not expect me to be a brain surgeon. My grandfather, told me one time, "I don't care what you do, you could be a ditch digger, you just be the best ditch digger there ever was." It wasn't a matter of having an expectation for me to be a lawyer or a doctor or whatever we may deem to be the most prestigious positions on the planet. Quite frankly I think being a pastor is about the most prestigious position every created by God. So I'm comfortable with where I'm at and with what I'm doing. But my parents just wanted me to do the best I could. When I messed up, it wasn't a matter of being a bad person. It was a matter of, "You're better than that!"

See, sometimes people respond with, "Let's beat you down," While some people respond with, "You know what? You are literally better than that. We don't do stuff like that!" Remember in the days when everybody used to have lines cut into their hair with clippers? They'd have them going all the way around their head and stuff like that. My grandparents, would babysit me during the day and I remember talking to my grandma one day.
I said, "All the kids got these lines in their head and I want one."
She said, "What tribe do you belong to?" I said, "What do you mean 'what tribe do I belong to'"?

My grandmother was half Indian, so she wasn't playing. She said, "What tribe do you belong to?" I said, "I don't belong to a tribe." She said, "Then you don't need lines on your head either do you?" Now some of you may think, "That was a little harsh." She was telling me, "That's not what we do. Everybody else can do that."

I'm not conceited; I'm confident; there's a difference. I understand who I am in Christ and I think some of you need to recognize who you really are in Christ. Paul told Timothy to not let anyone despise his youth. Timothy pastored the Ephesian church. He was a young man and the people were attacking him because of his age. But they failed to recognize that it wasn't a matter of him being old enough, it was a matter of him being excellent and doing things the way God would have wanted them to be done. There are a few theories of Timothy's age ranging everywhere from around twenty on up to his early thirties. It doesn't matter because Timothy pastored the largest known church in the world at that time. Can you imagine pastoring the church that Jesus' mother went to? The Apostle John went there, the one whom Jesus loved. Can you imagine preaching to them?

The criticism that could have come from all of that. Timothy was afraid, but he still had an excellent spirit. You can have fear and still be excellent. Timothy is pastoring the largest known church in the world, yet and still Paul had to put him there because Paul had a vision and he understood it. He knew that one man couldn't do it all. If you have a God size vision, you can't do all of it by yourself. If you can; it is not a God vision. When God gives a vision, it employs the masses. You can always tell the people who don't have a vision because they can't be excellent. They don't know where they're going or what they're doing, i.e. a lack of vision.

Restraint is a good thing. You ever heard, "The love of God constrains you?" Sometimes the love of God will keep you from doing some things. You know what I'm talking about; Sister Bucket-Mouth starts running her mouth and all of a sudden you like, "Really? You know, really?" There's that point where you become stressed. Then all of a sudden the love of God comes in and the mind overrides the body's desire to choke somebody. People who have no vision can't be excellent. They don't know what they're doing, they don't know why they're doing it and that's a sad thing. You ask somebody, "Hey where are you going to be in five years?" If they can't really answer that question right off the top of their head, they don't have a vision. That's why Paul said, "I press toward the mark of the high calling of God."

That word, "mark" in the NIV is translated as a "goal." A goal is a piece of your vision. I understand there's a vision and in order for me to accomplish the vision; I have to step through a series of goals to get there. But if I don't have a vision then I can't have a goal. If I don't have a goal, then you are accomplishing what your goal really is, which is nothing. The worst thing in the world is somebody that doesn't have a vision. Second worst is somebody who had the correct one and then someone else gave them another one.

God is looking for your fruit. The Bible says you know a person by the fruit they produce. If I put you in an orchard and I neglected to tell you what type of trees were there, you wouldn't know until you saw the fruit. People produce fruit and an unripe piece of fruit can still come off the tree. Not all fruit is sweet and good. I had a house that had an ornamental orange tree. If that isn't one of the stupidest ideas I ever heard in my life. Still have to pick the oranges, they still rot on the ground but yet they're ornamental which means you don't eat them. What is the point of that? It produced and looked like real oranges; cut one open you'll see it isn't. You have to realize that excellent people, they don't produce bad fruit. They'll tell you flat out, If my name's going to be associated with this; this has to be done right. I don't partner with people that don't share my values. I don't care if you're making a million dollars a day, if we don't have the same core values then I'm not interested. I'm not ruled by money; I'm ruled by God. I am reminded by a Hip Hop song that came out many years ago called CREAM it was an acronym that I have re-coined as "Christ Rules Everything Around Me." Whatever my name is associated with can not be junk. Sometimes you see professional athletes will do an endorsement deal strictly based on the money. I don't take anything because of the money. If it's not excellent I don't want anything to do with it. If it's not the best, my name doesn't go on it because I hold myself to a different standard.

Do you hold yourself to a different standard?

Do you recognize that you have to have a vision?

Do you recognize that God is the ultimate fruit inspector?

Do you recognize that everything you do, God is watching how you do it?

It's funny when people say, "I'm just volunteering. If you'd pay me, boy I'd give you everything." No, you won't. Over the years, I've hired people that made six dollars an hour to over six figures a year. Let me tell you something, a bum is a bum. They're a bum at two hundred thousand and they're a bum at six bucks an hour. It doesn't matter what you get paid. If you're moved by the money, you have no vision. I've never worked for money, never. I've taken jobs where I was paid very little, way less than what I'm worth. Let's be honest, who is really paid what they feel they're worth anyway? I work for opportunity. It has to do something for me; it can educate me.

My dream is to one day work at a pizza shop. I just want to learn how to make pizzas. I'd do it for free, I just want to learn. I value education more than money. "Pastor, if you'd pay me I'd come work for the church." That's why I won't pay you. I refuse because I worked for the church I pastor now for almost three years and never got paid. Served and worked for the church, that I came up in for eight years and never requested a paycheck. If you do it for the money, you're the wrong person because if you had a vision you would say this, "I know that if I bring my supply, I can make this organization better. If I make this organization better and increase it, God will take care of me financially. " That's faith!

But we'd rather go and sell ourselves to the highest bidder, when the real highest bidder is our Father. Listen, it's not for everybody, I know that. Could you imagine if I showed up to the church without my notes or my Bible? "Everybody, hold on I have to drive home and get my stuff." You would be irritated..

You expect me to be excellent because you know I have responsibilities. Yet you don't have a shepherd without sheep. Sheep have the same responsibility to show up as the shepherd does. We have what is known as a synergistic and a symbiotic relationship. I need you and you need me, that's how it works. People expect me to be excellent and some have no problem telling me when they think that I'm not excellent. We're still working on them. However, some are all too quick to have lunch and dinner and talk about how not excellent their leader really is. But do you hold yourself to the same standard?

Did you ever stop and think what we could do if five people said, "I'm going to go above and beyond." If you understand going the extra mile then that means for everyone there is two. I love addition; I really do. "One plus one equals two" is great, but when it comes to my finances I'd prefer multiplication. What if ten or twenty of us would say, We're going to give this thing thirty days of everything that we have. Can you imagine the progress that could be made?

I read a story about a guy who started a church in England. I believe He had three friends; two of them were doctors and the other a lawyer. They went to him and said, "God told us to quit our jobs and to put all of our money into this church." Now listen to me, I'm telling you a story, I am not telling you to do such a thing, I'm just sharing a story. If you do any such thing without having heard from God and all your life falls apart, do not blame me because I did not tell you to do

this. They wrote the article because these three men became millionaires. They asked them, "How did you get that way?" They said, "God told us to quit our jobs, take all that we had, and put it into this church. As we grew the church, God brought us businesses and companies because He knew we would put it into the organization."
They grew the church and God blessed them to such degree that all three became millionaires. These were not ignorant men or people that were easily deceived. They were highly educated people, those that have gone to graduate school. They heard the voice of God resounding in their hearts that said, "If we would just bring our supply..." How far would our organizations go if we had five people that said, "I'm going to bring my supply"? What if we have ten? How about twenty? Where would we be if thirty; how about if forty said, "We're going to bring our supply?"

The leaders that are over ministries in the church are all wanting to get people to serve in this capacity. Some of the leaders, they're working twice as hard. What if we brought everything we have? Not just on Sunday. What if we brought it throughout the week? Think of the people's lives we could affect and touch. Think of the things that we could do as the body of Christ. What would happen if we became the resource to feed and house people? What would happen if the city, the county, the state you're in, was looking at your church and asking you to help fix community and socio-economic problems. Do you think we'd be doing ministry for real then? I think we need to stop playing in the church! I'm talking about real ministry, but how do we get there? How do we get into the real that God desires? Do you think that He's sitting on high watching the things that are going on as we're flipping through the stations going, "Wow, that's a tragedy; somebody should do something about that. How could God let this happen in this world?" God isn't letting it happen; you are!

I'm passionate about this because I've seen the redemptive revelation and vision that God has. We all have heard, I hope; the speech that Martin Luther King Jr. gave called "I Have A Dream." If you haven't heard it recently, I want you to listen to it. I don't want you to watch it; I really want you to listen to it. You'll hear a cadence in his voice, almost like music. It's composed with such eloquence. I believe it's one of the greatest speeches ever given. He's describing a redemptive revelation that God gave him of what it was supposed to be. At the time, everyone thought he was crazy and it would never be like that. Racism still exists it's just a little more underground, so maybe it won't happen in our lifetime because it did not happen in his. Yet God gave him a vision that was not in his lifetime. He was merely a person that God used to get it to the next goal. The vision he had was not for right then, it was something to be aspired, to desire after, to chase after and to pursue because God gave him a vision. You need to have something to work towards. You need to see the end. For me, it's hard now because it's a double-edged thing. I want to know where I'm going, but yet once you know where you're going, sometimes you become agitated that you're not getting there fast enough.

You really become agitated when you begin to realize that it's not because you won't go; it's because someone else won't go. That's what caused Moses to strike the rock instead of speaking to it— the frustration of dealing with people. If God just wanted me to be there right now, he would have given me something I could do by myself, but He wants every one of you to see the vision and say, "I see that and we can get there. We might not get there in my lifetime, but I'm going to leave enough growth and advancement that my children can pick something up and continue on with it. There will be a value to my life that I will not just have been a blip on the radar, but that I'll have been a force to have been reckoned with. I will be known for having done something and I'll have a legacy that I can leave to my children and my children's children. I will know that my life counted for something because I have a vision and I'm excellent."

Chapter Eleven:
The Art of Vision

In business, they teach you that if you want to negotiate, one of the first rules of negotiation is to separate the people from the problem. By that I mean when a situation becomes tense; people have a tendency to start fighting with one another. Business is not personal; it's business. So the first thing you have to do is separate the people from the problem- otherwise you cannot come to a healthy resolution in anything. The second thing is you need to find out why they're making their decisions. You have to look for their core values of why they are choosing the position they have taken.

This is why dating can be so dangerous. Who you meet is not the person that you are really dating; you are meeting their representative, their front man, the person who they want to portray themselves as. There comes a point in time where you begin to learn what the core values of that person are, and this is what allows them to choose what they really want. They can tell you that they want something, but if their core values are off, then you don't really get to know who the person truly is.

The spirit of excellence should be so deep-rooted in you that it begins to color all your decisions, to color the choices you make concerning the people you allow to be in your life. What you tend to do just as in a relationship, is to date somebody based on the outside, what you can see but not recognize what's really on the inside. By the time you find out what's on the inside, sometimes it is way too late. You have to recognize who a person is on the inside, which means that you should first know who you are on the inside. You attract people who are like you, so if you don't like the person, then you better check who you are.

Everything has to have a vision. If you want to have a successful relationship, you better have a vision of what that's supposed to look like. I think it's the worst thing in the world for a father to have a daughter and not teach her how a man is supposed to treat her. She gets excited because the guy bought her a happy meal. If I have a daughter and you decide to date her, you better come with your checkbook because she's going to have expensive taste and if you don't think she's worth it, keep it moving. I wouldn't want her to be moved only by a man's financial ability but to make sure that it is part of the total equation. Romance without finance is a nuisance. It's a sad state of affairs that people don't understand these things. You've got to have a vision. A vision will answer the question, What do I really want in my life?

Do you have a vision for your family? Whether you're getting married, or you are married with kids, whatever the case may be. Where is your family going to be in five and ten years? Don't get mad when the kids are rebelling because they don't know where they're going. When the spouse is spending all the money because they don't know why they're saving. You need a vision and the vision is always given to the house. If you are the head of your house then God will give you the vision for where that home is supposed to go; what God wants from you and what He needs you to accomplish through your home. If you don't have a vision, Proverbs 29:18 tells us that "...for a lack of vision my people perish..."

It's the same thing with a business. The CEO has to have a vision of where the company is going. Why invest your life into something if nobody knows where you're going? A boat can rock and not go anywhere. Motion does not create effectiveness. I can sit in a rocking chair and rock myself silly, but I have not moved from the same spot. Motion does not equal momentum.

Everything must have a vision. The church universal has a God vision. The vision of our church was given to me. It is not to be swayed or influenced by anyone else other than God who gave me the vision. You have to be careful because people will come into the church with their vision and try to force their vision. That's a problem because the fastest way to steal somebody's vision is to give them another one. The vision is very fragile; the direction is very fragile. If you don't think direction is fragile, let's talk to the captain of the Titanic. Direction is very important, isn't it? Having your fingers on the pulse of what's going on around you is very important.

People who are of excellence, the first thing they will recognize is the vision of the house. The vision of the house is what guides and leads us, and it is what takes us where we're going. But when you deal with people, particularly in the church environment, they tend to jump from place to place. There's no loyalty to the church that God put them in so everything else that goes on, they run to it. That's a challenge for an excellent person because they see that there's a vision of the house in which God placed them in. They have to see that vision first before they have one of their own. Why? If God put you there, He put you there not for your vision, but for the vision of the house. We see in the Bible if people had a different vision and they came against their leadership, they walked off the pages of the Bible. Miriam was struck with leprosy and Barnabas sailed right off the pages of scripture. You don't hear from him ever again. The first characteristic of a person of excellence is they are able to see and to discern the vision. They know it, they see it, and they get it. The saddest thing in the world is to keep trying to cast vision to people who don't see it. Often it's really not that they can't, but they won't. They won't because they see it through the colored lenses of their own desires.

I was in the optical business years ago, in high school actually. I was an optician. I started out filing papers and when one of the opticians walked out the manager looked at me and said, "You want to learn how to make glasses?" I said, "Hmm, file papers or make glasses… Sure, let's do that!" Opportunity came because I was excellent. I did not dress like everybody else. I was sixteen years old, but I dressed sharp. When I came in, although I was filing papers, I came in like I was running the place. It's just my nature; it's my way of doing things. But here's my point, they gave me an opportunity based on the fact that I was there when an opportunity opened up. Most people miss an opportunity because their vision is messed up; they're too blinded by what "they" want. What if I'd have just said, "Look, I'm just here so I can buy gas for my car so that I can go party!" No, I wasn't there for that, I was there for promotion. If God opened an opportunity for me, I wanted it. I wanted everything I could possibly do and be the best that I could be, period. So when the opportunity came, they said, "Do you want to do this?" I said, "Sure I'll do it." They taught me and at the age of sixteen, now I am making great money. Anyway, in the optical lab we used to do tints in different colors. If you were a shooter, for example, one of the best colors to have in your glasses as a shooter is yellow. It gives you a greater degree of visual acuity. The worst color to have is polarized grey because it can be too dark. Now if you're a fisherman, that's a better color to have because it blocks out the light reflections on the water. Depending on the type of lens that you had would determine how much you could see. It's the same thing with vision. If you're tinted with a color of your own self and what you want and what you desire, then you will be colored against whatever the vision of the house is. If your vision is antithesis of the house, you won't be able to see anything. That's when you'll go into criticism and yield yourself to a critical spirit, "I don't understand why they do it this way. Why can't they do it that way? Why do we have to be here at this time? Why do we have to do this?" All these things are signs that you don't see the vision.

Excellent people can catch the vision very quickly and want to know what their part is. They know that if there's going to be a problem it will not happen on their watch, in their department, or their area of responsibility. That is just who they are. It is like a fish in water; there are certain things that should be innate to you. If you're a person of excellence, then you instinctively strive for the high mark.

In the local church, we recognize that everyone has a responsibility for the house. The house is not my house; it is the house that God has made me responsible for. He has a vision for this house. You'll always have people that say, "At our old church we used to..." Then go back. If it was so great, what are you doing here? "Well, I'm from Florida and over there this is how we do it." Go back to Florida because it is not where your from, it's where you are that counts. Be where you're at! Why are you in Arizona complaining about Arizona? It doesn't make any sense does it? There is something different and unique about every single place, every church, and every business. They all have unique characteristics and qualities and a person of excellence can fit in anywhere and do exactly what is necessary to bring increase to that body. The Bible tells us that we are all fitly together, joined together for the purpose of one thing— to make increase to the body. You have got to ask yourself when you come to church, do you make increase? Do you bring a supply? Because if you're a person of excellence, the first thing you'll ask yourself is, "Am I making any increase to the body? Am I doing anything that furthers the body or am I just here taking up space?"

"It pleased Darius to set over the kingdom an hundred and twenty princes, which should be over the whole kingdom; And over these three presidents; of whom Daniel was first: that the princes might give accounts unto them, and the king should have no damage. Then this Daniel was preferred above the presidents and princes, because an excellent spirit was in him; and the king thought to set him over the whole realm. Then the presidents and princes sought to find occasion against Daniel concerning the kingdom; but they could find none occasion nor fault; forasmuch as he was faithful, neither was there any error or fault found in him."
Daniel 6:1-4

Notice it did not say there was no fault in him, it just says there was not any to be found. People who are of excellence, it's not that you don't have problems or you don't have faults; we all have faults, problems and challenges. It is the one that is blithely unaware of their weaknesses that does not know how to mitigate their inabilities. The greatest philosopher ever, in my humble opinion, was Clint Eastwood. He said that a man must know his limitations. If you know what your limitations are then people of excellence begin to do whatever it takes to sure up their weaknesses. For as much as, he was faithful. Being full of faith is not the same as being faithful. You can be full of faith, among other things, and not be faithful. Faithful means you show up. Not only do you physically show up, but you mentally show up because you're in the game. Faithful people bring everything they have. It says that they could find no occasion nor fault. It does not say he did not have any, they just could not find them. Now, we have people saying, "You'll just have to accept me for who I am." What if who you are stinks?

What happened to excellence? What happened to "maybe I'm not perfect at it, but I'm going to keep working at it. I might be making small steps, but I'm going to make a step. I might not be moving as fast as everybody else, but I'm going to keep advancing forward."

There's a victorious mentality, a conqueror in you, and you have to learn how to stir it up. What happened to those that will stand up and say, "I might get beat today, but the sun shines on a dog's behind every once in awhile; and there is always tomorrow"?

He had faults; they just couldn't find them. But in the book of Daniel it says that they sought occasion against him. Every time you're excellent at something, someone will seek occasion against you. They're called haters, and haters are the breakfast of champions. The more haters I have, the better I know I'm doing. I want a league of haters; I might hire them and put them on payroll if I could, just to sit around and hate. I take that and I do business with it. If people aren't talking bad about you, if everybody likes you, you better "check yourself before you wreck yourself". You are going to offend people when you're working in excellence. They sought occasion against him because Darius was going to set him over the whole kingdom. He was going to be the number two man and they knew it. Their job was to do what? Make sure the king suffered no damage. It says out of all of them, a hundred and twenty princes, Daniel was the one of the three presidents that was over them and was keeping all the affairs in order. Why is that necessary?

Your leader can't do it all. This is why God brings people to the church, for them to do something, but then you find small-minded leaders that are afraid or threatened by someone who does better than they do. If I could find somebody that I know God has called to pastor this church and they'd do a better job than me, I am done. I don't want me; I want what God wants. I want excellence, the best possible. I want my church fed with the best food they could possibly have and if there's a better chef out there that can cook a meal better than me, I'm moving to the side.

I'm not threatened by anyone else. What God put in you is not in anyone else. You run around in fear, "Man, they're doing really good and they might take my job... Then what am I going to do?" What you're going to do is become promoted if you handle it right. I learned something in corporate America. You will never get promoted if there is not someone to take your job. You can either use it to your advantage or you can resist it, fight it and end up unemployed. I used to try and find my next replacement and train them in everything they needed to know because I knew the moment they could take my job, I'm ready to be promoted.

They were not happy with Daniel because the king is thinking about setting him over everything. Isn't that like people to be upset when you're about to get promoted? "I've been at the church longer, how come I didn't get promoted?" You're not excellent. We have to fight with you about what time you show up and argue about policy and procedure. You're not excellent; that's why and they sit.

"Shouldn't we just be fair?

If they got promoted shouldn't I..."

"No."

"Well, how come?"

Because you're not excellent.

Now it doesn't mean they can't be excellent, but at the moment they are not displaying what excellence should bring to the table. What does excellence do? It makes sure that those over you suffer no damage. That's excellence; that's how you know. It's not by what you say, it's not by how sharp you look. You could be as sharp and clean as the board of health but if you're not excellent, it shows. People can see it; it comes across in your attitude, your personality and how you leave your work. Excellent people don't leave work undone. I don't care if everybody walks out; I'm still going to make it happen. One monkey doesn't stop the show. Two monkeys don't stop the show either. We got to do what we got to do, plain and simple, "We git-r-done!"

There were nights where I would be up until 4 o'clock in the morning working on a project that my pastor sprung on me the day before service and ask, "Do you think we can get this done?" I'd say, "Yup!" I'd walk away from him and think, "Oh God, how are we going to get this done?" I did not walk in Sunday morning saying, "Here's what you asked me for; I was up until 5 o'clock in the morning!" I walked in, handed it to him and that was it. Sometimes he'd ask, "Was it difficult?" I did not bore him with the details or make myself appear heroic by explaining how hard it was. I was not going to tell him that because I understood that I was not doing this just for him, I was doing it for God. If he asked me for it, then God asked him for it and He asked me. I understand that I can recognize that it came from God. If I could do it for him, then I'm doing it for the one that sent him. I understood my responsibility to God and I feared God more than anything, but I also understood what the responsibility was. Why? I've run companies before and I know there are no trolls. If I don't get the job done, it doesn't get done. Plain and simple.

I have this "problem", and it's called "the gift of discerning of spirits", where I can come into contact with somebody and I just do not like them. They've done nothing, haven't said anything, I just do not like them. There is a rub. I remember, years ago, I was talking to my spiritual father and I said, "Dad, what's going on? Am I being judgmental? There are some people I simply do not like. They just rub me the wrong way. Why does that happen?" He said, "Here's part of the challenge, the Holy Ghost in you will come in contact with people and their spirit is just not right. When they're not right, they will rub you the wrong way. Now you've got to learn how to love people anyway and help them as long as they want to be helped until that changes. But you will come in contact with people that before they even say a word, you will already know."

Daniel had an excellent spirit in him and it always rubbed people the wrong way. Just in the same way that if another excellent person came up to him, you can tell. You can just see that, in people, they're excellent in how they carry and handle themselves. They're excellent about everything. If you think you're excellent at work but at home you're not excellent, you're not excellent. You're going to be excellent in every area of your life because it's just who you are.

These men were responsible for looking after the king's affairs, which means the king had to trust them. There are things that have to be done in the church and your leaders have to be able to trust people to do it. They can not put you over a ministry and have you arguing with everybody and allow people to leave out the door in droves because of your personality. I need people who understand excellence and how to deal with other people. If you can't deal with other people, you can't help me. Why?

Ministry is people; it's all about people!

If you say, "I'm just going to go into that ministry where I'll just preach and never have to deal with people." Help me find that ministry and I will be your first employee; because that's not ministry. Ministry is all about people; people that are hurting, people that are broken. It's all about seeing God restore their lives! If I was in this for the money I'd go back to corporate America and make fifty times what I'm making now. That's not an exaggerated statement, but I'm not about the money.

I want to see people's lives change. I want to see people go from where they were a year ago and develop to where they are today. I want to see real change that means more to me than any paycheck. I've had money longer than train smoke, and I've been broke. Let me tell you something; I'd rather have no money and see everybody successful than to have a boatload of money and wonder why am I here on this planet. Money doesn't change anything; affecting lives does and that's what we do. That's why we are fought so hard. We are not preaching candy-coated messages. We're not sending people through pomp and circumstance, with no disrespect to our other brothers in other denominations, but some of them, it's an aerobic show. There's no truth being taught and no word being preached.

In the time in which we're in, how are we going to make it if we don't have a group of people that are willing to stand up and say, "I'm going to be excellent, I don't care what the critics are going to say and I'd rather them criticize me for being the best, then criticize me for being the worst?" Both will draw criticism just the same, but one, I get rewarded and the other one I don't. God has a plan and a purpose for each and every one of you, He has a calling for each and every one of you and you better understand that you have to be excellent with that. You've got to know how to function and how to operate in ways that you're always bringing a supply to God's house.

"And Pharaoh said unto his servants, Can we find such a one as this is, a man in whom the Spirit of God is? And Pharaoh said unto Joseph, Forasmuch as God hath shewed thee all this, there is none so discreet and wise as thou art..."
- Genesis 41:38-39

Discretion is your ability to handle sensitive situations. Some people are about as discreet as a bull in a china shop and call it, "I'm just keeping it real." No, you're keeping it real stupid. Everything that is shared with you concerning the vision is not for you to reveal. There's a point where you need discretion. One of the reasons why Joseph was promoted was because he came before Pharaoh and he was discreet. Pharaoh could see that, in him, he understood how to handle himself in delicate situations. He was able to discern what's really going on. It blows my mind how people can be in such delicate situations and not know they're playing with a time bomb. You have to be a person of discretion. You've got to know that some situations are very delicate. "How come Pastor won't deal with so-and-so?" Because they have some challenges that I'm not willing to tell you about, but I believe that they're getting it together and whether it takes them a year, ten years or fifty years, until God tells me to deal with it, shut-up shutting-up. It's that simple. Because see, I can't reveal everything that I know because I understand discretion.

You tell some people things and it's around the church before the next Sunday. Now, a person of discretion knows that there are some things that if I want it to go around the church then they'll tell that person. A person of discretion knows how to handle those types of individuals. When you are wise and discreet, you're a person who can perceive the situation you're in, judge it correctly and then respond correctly. What you do is watch people like that. If you're in leadership and wondering who the next leader is, watch them in situations. If everybody knows their business, they're not discreet. I call them sunflower Christians. You know why a sunflower is called a sunflower? It's because whatever direction the sun is coming from, the flower will turn towards it to get all the sunlight. They run around telling everybody their problems, their challenges; wherever the attention will come from. The problem is there's no discretion in that. Some of you have been betrayed by people, but you were betrayed because you told them something you shouldn't have. Now whether you want to agree or not, it is true. If you had judged their character better, you would have never let them into that place to hurt you. Betrayal only comes when someone who is in the inner circle is able to betray you.

Acts 6:3 says, "…they were looking for men who were full of the Holy Ghost and of good report…" The people they needed to serve in the church were those that had a good reputation and could hear from God. Why do you need to hear from God? You need to have discretion to discern the situation you're in.

I was out to dinner one time with a couple and the waiter was just about as rude as they come. The wife said, "Maybe he's having a bad day." When he came back, I said, "Hey, is everything okay?" He began to tell me a story; his wife was diagnosed with cancer and given a very short time to live. It's taken everything he had and he's working multiple jobs to try to pay for all the medication and treatments. As he began to explain the story to me, it showed me one thing; that I need to ask myself better questions when people act certain ways. I was ready to cloud up and rain all over him, but I would have missed a God moment. That opened the door for us to pray with this man.

See, you have to have the Holy Ghost to be able to stop and hear. That's why he said, "I need people full of the Holy Ghost." I don't care if you can keep these floors clean; I need to know, can you hear from God? Do you have discernment? An excellent spirit will not cause damage! An excellent spirit will always seek to edify, seek to build, seek to restore and seek to repair.

One of my favorite lines is, "Problems is what I do." I solve problems; I'm good at it. I can come up with solutions, but that comes from years of problem solving. You know what management is? Management is removing other people's problems and excuses. What do some workers do? Some will come in, "I can't work today because my light bulb's out." You better get on the phone with facilities and get that light bulb replaced. They're always looking for a reason not to show up and managers are always looking to remove those reasons before they show up.

Excellent people understand discretion and wisdom. These are absolute characteristics of people who are excellent. They know how to function; they handle themselves well. The Bible says David handled himself wisely in the presence of Saul. He knew Saul was trying to kill him, but he behaved himself wisely. He wasn't out there getting loud and drunk acting a fool and drawing attention to himself.

"When wisdom entereth into thine heart, and knowledge is pleasant

unto thy soul; Discretion shall preserve thee, understanding shall keep thee...
- Proverbs 2:10-11

When knowledge or information comes in, how you handle it will keep and preserve you. How you process that information is what makes you different from other people. Some people can look at a situation and get right to the heart of it while others look at it and they're perplexed. They have fifty million questions, "But why? Why is this and what's that?" They have then encumbered you with a barrage of questions. If you have a person of excellence, you don't have a lot of questions. There's a certain discernment of the situation and you're able to fall into synergy with others. Paul said, about Timothy, "I have no one else who's likeminded that would naturally care for your state." In other words, Timothy was naturally like Paul. He did not have to waste time beating Timothy to knock the bad habits out of him. What Paul had to do was put in Timothy what he needed to be successful, then step back and let him do it.

When you find excellent people, all they need is to be equipped; they don't need to be beat. Give them what they need and step out because they have discretion and understanding. If you have information, you should be able to pull something out of it. That's what makes you excellent. You get it when others don't. You see it when nobody else sees it. That's what sets you apart and makes you so noticeable.

Sometimes when I meet with people for a development meeting, I'm listening to figure out, "Do they get it?" If I hear that they "get it", I invest more of my time. When I do not think they are yet ready, I back off because I cannot move any further until they've grown. I cannot bring revelation; only God can, but I know when I hear revelation being spoken. I know it because I hear what they're saying as well as what they're not saying. It's all about excellence.

If you have a company, the people you should choose in your company are people that keep you from suffering damage. If you are always getting hit by the people around you because the bullets keep flying passed them, at some point in time you have to stop and say , "Wait a minute, isn't it your job to hold this shield? Why do I keep getting hit? Why is the king suffering?" There are things that I should not have to put my mind to. If you want a word that comes from study, it takes a long time to come up with the messages that I preach to you. I don't preach garbage, I preach my best and I study my best. That takes time, energy and effort. Do you think I really can run around here and sweep every floor, talk to every person, shake everybody's hand and kiss every baby? It's not possible. That's why God brought you, so you can shake every hand, kiss every baby, tell everybody how much "your leader" loves them.

My job is to feed the sheep, not to be your best friend, socialize with you or be your pal, but to feed you what God wants you to have. That's my job and the measure of my success is not based on whether or not you feel warm and fuzzy with me, it's whether or not you're growing as a Christian.

It agitates me to no end when people say, "I don't know if people want to hear the truth so maybe that's the problem." What am I going to do, stop preaching it? You think I'm going to seek their approval over His approval? I have a limited time with you and an eternity with Him. I'd rather Him be happy and you have a problem.

"Seest thou a man diligent in his business? He shall stand before kings; he shall not stand before mean men."
- Proverbs 22:29

He did not say "smart", he said diligent. What is a diligent man? A diligent man is someone who will not give up. They stay after it; on it morning, noon and night. They put their hand to the plow and keep their hands there. They're not the ones who take a smoke break every fifteen minutes.

I'll never forget this guy that I hired as an engineer because he was a little touched in the head. I did not know that when I hired him, but we found that out later on. So much so that when I fired him, I called my best friend at the time, gave him the guy's name, social security number, phone number and his address. I said, "If you hear anything on TV about somebody coming and shooting this place up, it was him." He would work on a computer a little bit, put it back, then he'd go to the bathroom and wash his hands. He'd be in there for a good 15-20 minutes washing his hands. Then he would come out and he'd grab another computer, work on that for 15-20 minutes, then go back in the bathroom again and wash his hands for another 20 minutes. This went on all day long so that the floor manager came in, he's like, "I don't know what we're going to do with this guy because he's not cutting it." Every time I walked through the floor, I'd see him and I'd watch him a little bit and see how he responds. Sure enough, everything the manager told me he was doing, this guy's doing.

He did not fit because he was not diligent. How could we pay him an hour's worth of work and not receive an hour's worth of work? He had the cleanest hands in the building and if he were a nurse or a doctor he'd fit in perfectly. Since our surgery was on computers, he didn't fit. When I started to tell him he did not fit, the first thing he said to me was, "You can't fire me for that!" I said, "We're a privately held company, I could fire you because I don't like your breath." Of course, I've grown a lot nicer these days. God is not through with me yet!

The hand of the diligent will always bring you in front of kings. You can catch diligence; you can see it. I walked my church sometimes and I know who's diligent; I can see it. I can see the ones that are making things happen and are on top of stuff. I can also see the ones that, as soon as I walk in, they go grab a broom. They make sure they sweep past me and it's the first time they touched a broom all day.

It's what you do when no one's looking that makes you diligent and the hand of diligent men will always bring you in front of kings. It's just a characteristic that we have to bring back because truthfully, in the generation that is coming up now; there's no excellence or honor. In twenty years, would you want some of this current generation changing your adult diapers if you were in assisted living facility?

Often times the response is if you'd pay me more, I'd be more excellent. That's a lie. If their goods can be bought, then I rank that very close to a level of prostitution. I can't be bought, I can be influenced. If you need my help I can bring my supply, but I can't be bought. Whether you pay me little or pay me a lot, if I told you I'm going to do it, I'm going to do it like you're paying me three hundred dollars an hour even if you're only paying me three dollars because that's just who I am. I can't be bought, can you?

Nobody's ever paid what they're worth, but for excellent people that's not their goal. It's not about money; it's about success and being a part of something greater than themselves. It's about having a commitment to something that makes a difference in this world and trusting that the money will always come. I never chose jobs based on money; I chose them based on opportunity, the product or the people that I got to work with and learn from is remarkable. You choose based on what is going to enhance, not just what will pay you. If you do it right and you trust God, you'll have more money than you know what to do with. We have to learn how to become people of excellence.

If you're going to get into ministry, you have to be excellent. If you feel like you're at a stand-still in ministry, you're not excellent because excellence will always garner promotion. Maybe you're excellent at this level. A rubber band is designed to be stretched. The problem with God's people is the moment they start to be stretched, they begin to complain and whine and murmur not realizing that you were designed for that purpose. A rubber band won't work until you stretch it; that's what it's designed for.

You're called to stretch. There will always be constant resistance when you stretch. There is an equal amount of force from both sides, but the one that wins is the side that's stronger. Everything in your life will be pulling you up and down at the same time and if you are a person of excellence, you will always be pulling up. You will not let it pull you down because a person of excellence says, "No, we're going to keep the bar here. If nothing less, we're going to maintain this standard."

The primal enemy of your best is "good enough." "Nobody will see those pieces of gum under the table so we won't worry about it. We'll just worry about the pieces of gum on top of the table." Until you get somebody like me. Sometimes the first thing I do when I enter a restaurant is check under the tables. That tells me whether I want to eat there or not. In ministry, if you're not excellent, Satan will find every weakness you have. If you have to be encouraged all the time, told how much you're appreciated and you need access to everybody and everything to complain and vent. Satan will use that to derail you. If you need a lot of attention, if you're a sunflower and you stop getting it, Satan will use that against you.

Some people came to our church and wanted to start a teen ministry. I knew that they were not ready for that. Later we ended up having to do marriage counseling. We uncover that there are issues and challenges. Do you think I'm going to let a teen girl around this man who's already having problems? I knew that before they said anything. I knew it by the Holy Ghost, but in their minds I am stifling their dream. No, I'm not stifling your dream, I'm helping you. I'm keeping your simple self out of jail. If I put you in the wrong situation and you do the wrong thing, you're going to bring reproach upon the ministry and yourself. It is our responsibility to operate and function in excellence because then we are beyond reproach. When you're beyond reproach, then there are no problems or issues that can be found in you. Doesn't mean you won't struggle, but it means that nobody can bring that out of you to cause problems.

Of course, they left because I really wasn't willing to give in to what they were asking for. Their last words were this, "We just have a different vision than you." That's like me walking into your house and saying, "Hey I know you painted this wall yellow, but I have a different vision for you." If I'm in your house, just feed me. Give me a vision for some ribs and some cornbread. Everything else, it's your house and you do what you need to do. Just like when I go to a church, all I want to do is be fed. If I know I'm being fed then I'm not going to eat until I get full, I'm going to eat until I get tired. Plain and simple because that's what we're here for.

People who are excellent have great understanding and discernment. When you have to spend a lot of time trying to get people to see the vision, at some point you have to let it go because their dead weight. You can't keep explaining yourself over and over again. They don't have discretion, wisdom, or understanding. I know you wanted me to tell you that we just work with everybody. We love everybody, but I won't work with everybody, because not everyone is excellent.

I want people to see excellence in everything we do. I want people to see Christ in it. When people come to the church you serve and all they should say is that the only thing missing in this place is me. This is why sometimes people are agitated with me because I expect the best. We're going to do the best, we have to. I don't know any other way to do it and that's what sets us apart from all the rest. That's what makes it so that people look at you and know that God's really working in our life. Otherwise, you'll be like those Christians out there drinking and partying until they fall on Saturday and then dragging themselves in (maybe) on Sunday. Their friends look at them and think, "You're no different than me." You have to applaud them because, at minimum, they decided, "I ain't going to church, I'm still trying to get my party on!" At least they don't want to be hypocrites.

Chapter Twelve:
The Art of Division

"Here a dinner was given in Jesus' honor. Martha served, while Lazarus was among those reclining at the table with him. Then Mary took about a pint of pure nard, an expensive perfume; she poured it on Jesus' feet and wiped his feet with her hair. And the house was filled with the fragrance of the perfume. But one of his disciples, Judas Iscariot, who was later to betray him, objected, "Why wasn't this perfume sold and the money given to the poor? It was worth a year's wages." He did not say this because he cared about the poor but because he was a thief; as keeper of the money bag, he used to help himself to what was put into it. "Leave her alone," Jesus replied. "It was intended that she should save this perfume for the day of my burial. You will always have the poor among you, but you will not always have me."
- John 12:2-8

Mary begins to anoint Jesus' feet with oil and Judas, who has oversight of the money, decides that he's going to speak up and ask why the oil was wasted. He felt that they should have sold it and given the money to the poor. Judas was not the leader and did not have all the information. Jesus, God in the flesh, had all the answers and all the questions. Yet and still, Judas felt it necessary to question Jesus. What he viewed was a gross misuse of ministry funds. Jesus clarifies the

195

situation by letting him know that Mary was preparing him for His burial. Jesus responded with, "The poor you'll have with you always." Jesus did not call him out and say, "You're not interested in the poor, you're just trying to steal the money." Jesus answered his statement with an appropriate response.

You have to be very careful when challenged in public because the court of public opinion can be very detrimental to a ministry. Jesus had enough wisdom to not throw stones at him, as this would have seemed defensive and could have diminished the impact of his response. Instead, he stayed with what Judas' response was and with wisdom shut him down. Almost as if to say, "Even if your concern was legitimate, you'll have the poor with you always." I believe this was a setup. Had Jesus flat out exposed him, I believe it would have been a problem. So Jesus skillfully responded to the issue on the table before everyone. Be careful how you respond to your critics in public; even when you know their intentions are less than pure. Divisive spirits always come to challenge and divide leadership. They will begin to do it in very subtle ways. They'll start asking about why things are done so meticulously. They butterfly around to different people, trying to find those they can convert into allies. They invite you to events and different things that are not hosted by your church. They're trying to see where you and your loyalties lie. Once they are able to discern that you could be loyal to them, then they become bolder with expressing their convictions and their statements. They begin to say more because they're planting seeds, seeds of division. It's not that it's wrong to support other ministries but your primary loyalties and support should be for the ministry God placed you in. You will grow where you are planted.

Judas would have done better if he'd have pulled Jesus aside and asked him why did this happen this way. Even though technically he still had no right to do that, it would have been better if he had done it that way. But he confronted Jesus in front of everybody and forced him to respond, yet Jesus never called him out. He could have easily said, "You're not interested in the money and you know that." So what happened?

Jesus had all power under total control. If you need to assert your authority in every situation, you don't have any. When people blow up, they become excitable, loud, boisterous... It's usually because of unresolved fear in their life, and are trying to cause intimidation in yours. The only reason why they're trying to intimidate anyone is because they are afraid and hold no authority or power, or at least that's how they see it. They tend to want it desperately, and it will cause them to say things that they should not say.

How did Judas become so familiar and comfortable with Jesus to the point where he found no problem with challenging Him in front of everyone? Why did he have no honor or think to himself that he may not have known why Jesus did it that way, but maybe he was on a need to know basis? People tend not to see the spirit of division that comes into them. It gets them to a place where they make the decision that they are going to challenge things. That's where it starts.

"As soon as Judas took the bread, Satan entered into him."
- John 13:27

This is the very next chapter where we see that the first onset is the challenging, and the questioning. It's okay to ask God questions, however, it's altogether a different story to question God. Those in leadership that are closest to me know why I do certain things, they understand how it affects certain individuals, how I'm careful about their feelings. I want to preserve relationships so sometimes I put up with stuff that I don't really want to, but I do it because I understand the individuals involved and I desire to keep them connected. That decision was made between the leader and God to do whatever is needed to be done. Therefore, the leader is not required to tell everything that goes on or why. They do have to be accountable. For example, I'm accountable to those that are above me in the Lord. If my spiritual father asks me, "Hey why'd you do that?" Then I offer him answers and explanations until he's reasonably assured that I'm operating within the fiduciary responsibility of what I have taken on.

But when you start to put yourself in a position where you begin to question things in a divisive way. That was the start for Judas. The next chapter it says Satan entered into his heart. How did Satan get into his heart? He opened the door. The Bible says, "Let not your heart be troubled." You can give your heart permission to be troubled and allow things into your heart, but it begins in the place where you have little or no respect, honor, understanding or discernment of how to handle yourself appropriately. Sometimes people can really call out a demon in somebody else, but they have a real hard time looking at the speck and the beam in their own eye. When you begin to challenge your leadership, the results tend not to be good. I am not advocating blind submission, but I am speaking about a healthy way to handle and resolve issues. Imagine the fact that Jesus, all the while knew that the one who was going to betray him was Judas.

Jesus, as the leader of the ministry, is watching Judas; recognizing his behavior and knows that he's the one that's going to betray him. All the while, Jesus never says a word, never calls him out, never confronts him, but he watches him. Once Satan entered into his heart, he said, "The thing you're about to do? Do it." Can you imagine the frame of mind to be sitting at a table and watch Satan enter into somebody? Then, to command Satan saying that which you're about to do, do it quickly.

Success leaves clues. When you see someone who claims to be successful you have to ask yourself, do they have anything that is the fruit of their success. Ladies when you meet a guy, if you're smart, the first thing you're going to do is look at his shoes. The second thing you're going to do is find out how generous he really is because if he's tight with his money, then he might not have any. Because success leaves clues. If you're successful, you'll have the things that successful people have. You'll carry yourself in a successful way and you'll dress in a successful way. So when you see someone that says, "I was this, that and the other..." But they don't have anything; odds are they never were. They don't have anything that shows there was ever any fruit from being successful. If they tell you they once had successful businesses and they're wearing a plastic digital watch that cost two dollars, you have to ask yourself, "If you really were all that successful, what did you do with your money?" In the same way that success leaves clues, so does betrayal.

You can look at people's behavior and know that person cannot be trusted. You can tell by how they handle situations. People want to get into ministry, but you never see them at church. Their attendance is erratic, they can't show up on time; they don't support what the church is doing, and they're out supporting everybody else's church. But they're not supporting the one they're at and then you wonder how they got this loose spirit. See, betrayal leaves clues. People who want to serve in the church but not willing to tithe to it are leaving clues. So the very organization in which they want to serve, they are not willing to support? But you'll ride off the backs of other people. See, betrayal leaves clues.

So when you watch people you think, "You know, Pastor's a little rough." Yeah, he is. You want to know why? Betrayal leaves clues and if you want to protect an organization you have to know how to watch the signs and the signals. I can easily discern when people get offended, their giving stops. Pridefully they will rob God and walk in poverty just to show me a thing or two. When we first started the ministry, just like anybody else, I was always concerned who the leading givers were. We had somebody, who is not at the church anymore, but they were a huge giver. They struggled with alcohol and I found myself sometimes touching that subject and then getting off of it very quickly. Then I came to the realization, I can't do that. I have to preach it the way God gives it to me. If they like it, they like it. If they don't, they don't. Well, I preached a message and I touched some subjects and within a few weeks the giving stopped and then their attendance stopped. It became sporadic, then eventually they were gone and so went their money. Immediately God brought in and raised up others and we never felt the loss.

I was in a meeting with someone one time and they said, "We're here because the kids need us. We have to stay because if we left, the church would fall apart." I told them, "Make sure you never forget this one thing, the church doesn't "need" you. They "need" God, this is not yours; this is God's. If you walked out today or tomorrow, God will send the right people to take care of his organization. Don't ever convolute your thinking by allowing yourself to believe that you are so important that things will not function without you."

Leaders have the desire to protect the organization because they're responsible for it. It's like laying people off. I've worked in C-Levels of companies where they did spreadsheet management. You look at a spreadsheet, you figure out who makes the most and if you fire these four people then I can hire ten. So guess what you do? You fire those four people and you hire five and you save the difference. What people don't realize is, let's say the company has a hundred people and they fire ten. The ten people are very upset that they lost their jobs, but what they don't know is that the CEO is responsible for the other ninety, as well. If they did not let go of the ten, every person in the business would be out of a job. Sometimes hard decisions have to be made in order to preserve the whole bunch.

Betrayal always leaves clues and it always starts with questioning. It always starts with what seems to be innocent challenging. "Well, I just wanted to know..." No, they did not, because if they really wanted to know, they would get involved in that ministry. They would serve and then find out what the challenges really are.

Then they would get their answers. Instead, what they want to do is sit on the outside and draw criticism against that which they don't participate in. Participation is what qualifies their opinion. Success always leaves clues; betrayal always leaves clues. We have to be able to recognize them because they are patterns and they're easy to see.

What we see in John 12 and 13 is that Satan oppressed him outwardly until he surrendered inwardly. I had enough sense that when I dealt with my pastor if I didn't understand why he did something, I did not say anything publicly. You want to know why? I do not like the taste of my foot. I've learned that there had to be a reason, and whether I knew it or not did not matter. As long as he was not doing anything illegal, unethical, or immoral then I had to give him the leeway to make decisions. I knew he had information that I did not have.

There is a satanic kingdom and it influenced the princes and the King of Tyre. Sometimes, people think a Jezebel is a loose woman. I want you to understand that a jezebel is not a just loose woman. A Jezebel is someone who does not want to be submitted to authority. Jezebel will tend to use sexuality as a manipulating force in order to give sway to leadership. People tend to see the sexuality aspect of a Jezebel, but they don't realize it's deeper than just looseness. It is manipulation.

Jezebel was the daughter of a pagan king. She was a Phoenician who worshiped the devil. She was given over in marriage to the king of the Northern Kingdom of Israel. It was a political maneuver to infiltrate into Israel. It was done to cement a relationship between that which was holy and unholy. It's one kingdom trying to use something to infiltrate another kingdom. It was the kingdom of darkness using bait to infiltrate the kingdom of righteousness; an offering of sorts. Here's what it does. Number one, it cements a relationship. Number two, it invades and infects the kingdom. Number three it turns the people of God away from God towards Satan. Jezebel, from the very beginning, was offered as a way to bring the people of God away from God. Equally important to remember is that you can not have a Jezebel without an Ahab. Jezebel came in the form of a wife that should have been a help meet, but in reality is a whole world of hurt for Ahab.

"There was never anyone like Ahab, who sold himself to do evil in the eyes of the Lord, urged on by Jezebel his wife. He behaved in the vilest manner by going after idols, like the Amorites the Lord drove out before Israel."
- 1 Kings 21:25-26 NIV

The name *Jezebel* means, "without husband or without head." It implies a lack of submission to the head that is over it. Jezebel cannot operate without Ahab. Its purpose is to remove authority, to remove the head, the organization and headship. It's to take off leadership so that there is no one in charge but Jezebel. It is not specifically delineated to just females. Jezebel's sole purpose was to usurp authority. She was given as a wife of submission and then she worked diligently to influence her husband to do vile things before God.

I'm sure all he thought was, "Wow, she's cute!" Not realizing that the weapon formed against him was now prospering. When you view this in light of the church, you can always spot the spirit of Jezebel working in people. For example, my assistant handles my calendar, period. I'll always have people that want to contact me directly instead of going through her. Jezebel must have a direct relationship with leadership and they are unwilling to submit to the process or structure. They're not doing it by accident; they're doing it because they do not agree with it. As far as my schedule goes, if you want me to show up then, you need to talk to somebody who's good at putting it on the calendar. I'll make an appointment, forget to calendar it, and subsequently forget to show up. There are reasons why certain people are placed in charge. There are people who are over the ushers for a reason. Do not come ask the pastor everything about that ministry, they usually don't know. People who struggle with this, they always want to be close and talk directly to the pastor.

"Why can't I have a relationship with the pastor? I don't see why I can't get to him." First of all, I don't know you. Second of all, you are not tried and tested therefore I don't need you next to me until I know who you are and what spirit you're of. Jezebel was offered to Ahab and she came in the form of a help meet. Someone that he should have been able to depend on. Yet her heart was not right.

There are people and they'll serve under someone who's ahead of a ministry and when the pastor is around they will act right but when pastor is not around, they give the head of the ministry a hard time. At times in my church, if I make a direct request of them they'll do it, but if I send someone to ask, they will not. They require a connection to the head because they cannot submit and if they can't get that connection, they get offended and they will then leave.

A few years back, we had someone coming to our church who caused all kinds of problems and havoc. Their doctrine was completely messed up, absolutely demonic! They left because they could not submit and did not want to change. They were offended that I did not chase after them to bring them back. First of all, I don't have to go after the wolves, I go after sheep. My responsibility is to protect the fold. I'm the one that has to give an account for your souls. I'm the one that has to answer for you, not to the wolf. "I just feel like I should be at a church where I can touch my pastor whenever I want to." Then go find that. But I can tell you one thing; you're not going to walk into any other church and grab the pastor before he has to preach to tell him about your bad grandchildren or your crazy child.

There is an anointing to be protected. They're not protecting the man; they're protecting the anointing on the man and Jezebel's spirit does not want that to happen. If jezebel can decapitate the head of the organization, then it cannot function. Listen, one man cannot do it all.

Jethro told Moses that he was going to have to need some help. There were three million Israelites; I am certain that they all wanted to speak to Moses directly. Organizational structure is important to success. If Judas had been submitted to Christ, he never would have asked that question. It wouldn't have been a thought in his head. He should've said, "I'm not sure what we doing here, but he usually tells us so I'm just going to wait and see."

Now the flip side of that is this, you can't have Jezebel without Ahab! You will find that most women who struggle with a Jezebel spirit will always pick a man who's one of two ways. They will always pick a man that is henpecked and will do whatever they say, when they say, and how they say. Or they'll pick one who has feminine characteristics. If he has feminine characteristics, then in their mind they are able to create equality in the relationship by becoming more masculine.

You will have people that will say, "Well, you know Pastor, my partner and I are equal." Yes, you are equal heirs in Christ and you are equally created, but there's a challenge here.

If I'm the President of the company and you're the Vice President, are we equally created? Yes.

Do we have different functions? Yes.

Does that make me better than you? No.

We are both heirs in Christ, but I have a different responsibility, don't I?

The man gives an account for his home whether he knows it or not. I wish some men would grow up and realize that they're going to be the one standing before God to give an account for their family. If you're running around trying to populate the world with little people that look just like you, you better wake up. Please know that I'm not saying one is more important than the other, what I'm saying is that man has a certain responsibility. What women under the influence of Jezebel tend to do is seek a level of authority and control in order to bring the leader into submission. Jezebel will try to stay close to the leader in order to influence him through suggestions and opinions. "Well, you know if it was me, this is what I would do." Nobody asked. You tell people, "This is how I want this done..." And they have fifty million ideas of how it should be done differently because they saw it somewhere else. They never took the time to figure out why we handle it that way. Then they will try to convince the leader that they are the only ones who can achieve something that a leader cannot do themselves to create dependance and reliance upon them.

I have seen people take over a company or division and the first thing they do is fire everybody. That's the worst mistake in the world because you don't know what's wrong, and the people you just fired are the only people that could tell you. So the first thing you learn in change management, is find out what's going on, then you fire the ones that need to be fired and promote the ones that need to be promoted. You do this based on assessment and evaluation, not a blind show of force. It is amazing to me how people will have so many opinions and know absolutely nothing about our organization. Their first time at the church and they have a million and one suggestions. If you haven't been here long enough, sit down for awhile and figure out what the church does and why they do it first. Then, come serve and learn more. But people don't want to do that. They want to come in with their "gift" and try to get directly next to leadership or they tend to choose people who don't understand authority or submission to buddy up with. They hate authority, hate being told what to do and hate being asked to arrive on time. They just do not want to do it. They do not want to be corralled or told what to do.

Listen, if you're ever going to be in a position of leadership, you cannot do whatever you want. If you cannot follow the man you can see, you'll never follow the God you cannot see. When you notice people who hate authority, you should keep a close eye on that person. Those that can handle authority, when they are told that this is the way I want it done then that's the way it's done. If you have a better suggestion, work in the ministry for awhile and submit your suggestions to your ministry leader. Your immediate leader is now responsible to submit it to the headship of the organization. If you find out it did not get to the top, then you have a valid complaint. However, don't go selling your idea to everybody, "You know I was thinking we should put better toilet paper in the bathroom. What do you think?"

A Jezebel tends to be very sweet until confronted. Very sweet, syrupy make-your-teeth-rot sweet. However, the moment they're confronted, they're explosive. In the real estate business, one of the unique things you have to deal with is termites. Every house either had termites, will have termites or currently has them; it's a very common problem. One time, I sold a house back East. The home inspector said he was up in the attic and he said he saw a termite peek around a corner and look at him. Here's the problem with that statement. First of all, the odds of him being able to see something that small in an attic are probably slim to none. However, termites have a very unique characteristic. They do not like light or air. When a termite is boring through wood, if it hits air and exposes itself, it will back up, patch up the hole and continue another direction. In a garage, you may see mud tubes coming down the concrete walls. They will completely conceal and encapsulate themselves from air. Since they cannot dig through the concrete block, they will create a tunnel and go over it.

Jezebel does not like to be exposed and will stop at nothing to remain clandestine. Psychology tends not to help because they're in complete denial. Usually, you cannot just sit down and confront them. In their minds, it doesn't exist. That's the danger of it.

They also will falsely accuse and find it very difficult to forgive. They often seek out weaker members in the church and they try to get them to follow them, so they have somebody to boss around. They have to bark out an order to somebody, so they'll find the younger ones and they'll "woo" them into following .They will build an entourage of people who support them. They will insert themselves as the one who loves the people and the leaders don't. They target people; they're very pointed in their targeting. They go after the ones that don't know any better. I don't mean that in a bad way, when you first come you begin to learn about your Christianity, you don't have a lot of understanding. They seek out the ones who don't have understanding because they know that the young ones in Christ do not know better.

When confronted, they will usually cycle between two personalities; victim and aggressor. They will usually start with the victim and when the victim does not get what they want, they will become an aggressor and attack. Remember, the spirit of Jezebel is not omnipotent, so they have to get close to you in order to study you and learn what your weaknesses are. They're the ones that want to come to your house and go out and fellowship. They want to stay very, very close to you because they're trying to figure you out.

When you're the leader, they tend to try to imitate you. They want to look like you, sit where you sit, and do what you do. What they're trying to do is experience being you. See, nobody can do you like you! A Jezebel spirit wants to be like the leader. But the problem is there's no way possible for them to do that. They're trying to steal the anointing on your life.

The anointing is not transferred by imitation; it's transferred by duplication. Duplication takes a concerted effort. We have CDs that we duplicate for our Bookstore. The original CD is put into a machine that duplicates it to another CD. That CD does not imitate the other CD, it's duplicated; it's a purposeful attempt. So in order for you to really have an anointing, someone has to take the time to duplicate in you what's in them. You can imitate me all day long. You can dress the way

I dress, get glasses like I have and drive the same car, but you will never be me. People really struggle with that, especially in the corporate world.

"Getting on his high horse one day, Korah son of Izhar, the son of Kohath, the son of Levi, along with a few Reubenites— Dathan and Abiram sons of Eliab, and On son of Peleth—rebelled against Moses. He had with him 250 leaders of the congregation of Israel, prominent men with positions in the Council. They came as a group and confronted Moses and Aaron, saying, "You've overstepped yourself. This entire community is holy and God is in their midst. So why do you act like you're running the whole show?" - Number 16: 1-3 MSG

The first thing Korah did was go after people who had positions. He did not approach Moses with a bunch of foot soldiers. He came with people who had influence. You've got to be very careful, especially leadership in the church because if they can't get to the pastor they're coming after the leadership to sway them against the pastor.

Here's what I call the "Me and JC routine." This is where people have no loyalties to the local body of Christ, the church, of which they're planted in. They believe it's just them and God. When they do not get their way... "Well God's moving me on." Listen, usually if the pastor does not know, and is not in agreement that God moved you on, God most likely didn't move you on. That doesn't mean you cannot move on, you certainly can. You have free will, but I'll tell you this much. You don't "went" you are "sent." It blows my mind when people say to me, "My assignment here is over and I'm moving on." Who told you that? It's a lack of submission because God will speak to everybody. Everybody will know it's your time, it'll be absolutely clear. The only person who might not know its your time is you. But everybody else will know because God will speak through the leadership.

Here, Korah is challenging Moses. God called Moses to run the show. He was the one sitting before the burning bush getting instruction and the one whom God revealed himself to as the I Am, not Korah. He's the one that God speaks to mouth to mouth while he speaks to everyone else in visions and dreams. Moses understood the ways of God, not just the acts of God. How dare Korah go before the man of God and say, "We have God too!" Really? Then go do what Moses did. Take yourself to Egypt and let His people go. They basically came to Moses and told him that he had too much power.

People will always volunteer to be at the highest level of the organization, but they are not always equipped to do the job. One of the sure signs of a Jezebel spirit is they will jump up and try to get involved at the highest level of the organization, not because they're capable, but because they desire influence. Can't do the job, and know they can't do it. Can't type worth a lick and they're the first one to offer, "

"Can I help you type?"

Can you type? "No."

"I want to play the piano."

Can you play the piano? "No."

Why do they do that? They're looking for influence. They're not looking to bring a supply to the organization— they're looking to get next to the leadership. They will quit when they do not get their way, or they will invite people in the church to events at their home privately because they think there's too much control other places particularly when it's not in their hands.

'It's God you've ganged up against, not us. What do you have against Aaron that you're bad-mouthing him?"
Numbers 16:11 MSG

They were swallowed up by the earth. They did not attack Moses; they came against God. God was the one who set it all up and anointed Moses and Aaron. Sometimes people are not coming against you; they're coming against what and who you represent. Remember, God told Samuel that the people were not rejecting him they where rejecting God. There are times where your anointing will get out in front of you and it will cause agitation. It will rub people the wrong way. You'll be minding your business, shopping in a store and people will have negative attitude towards you because the God in you agitates them. The world will reject the God in you.

Korah and these men are challenging Moses and God opened up the earth and swallowed them up. We have to be able to recognize rebellion in our own selves because even if it's in us, it doesn't mean we're Satan. It just means we've yielded to some things we shouldn't yield to. It started in Judas with oppression and then Satan entered into his heart because he kept yielding to it. All of us can be subject to that attack, but the only way you're going to know is to be circumspect about your behavior. How do you act? How do you handle authority? Do you like organizational structure or do you hate submission?

People have to understand proper boundaries when dealing with leadership. They have to be careful that it doesn't become about having access. You've got to be careful when you think like that. I'll send a message through somebody, "Go tell this person to do such-and-such..." They'll come back and say, "Well I told them, but..." Then I'll call the person directly and say, "Hey can you do this, that and the other?" "Oh sure, no problem!" Why couldn't they do it when I sent the message? They hate organizational structure. That's why the earth swallowed them up. They did not want Moses anymore. They wanted, "Just me and JC."

I see people who go to Bible College and they have more regard for the college they're going to than what they're getting in their local church. Bible college does not qualify you for ministry. You can go to a Bible College and read every book until your ears look like book covers. You will not be qualified for ministry because you attend college; it's by the anointing. So now, is attending college a good idea?

Of course! Just make sure you go to one that teaches the truth. When you get into ministry, it's amazing how many people are not told these things. So they come out of school ten foot tall and bulletproof. They get into an organization and wreak havoc because they think, "Well I've got a degree." I don't care if you have more degrees than a thermometer, you need more than just a degree; you need common sense. You need an anointing and good character, but people don't want to submit to that process.

I tell people, "Hey! Sit, relax... Just grow, learn and develop." "Well can I preach?" No. "Can I..." No, you can go over there and help with the Ushers. You can come in here and sweep the floors. "But I'm called to be a prophet to the nations."Well, prophesy that broom into your hands and start sweeping. There's a process of development and growth that has to be followed. Unfortunately because they don't want to sit under the fathering process. We end up having a bunch of fatherless children running around trying to figure out how to find a home. They go from church to church, place to place and pastor to pastor with their "gift."

Everybody is a prophet nowadays. I always wonder, "How come God is able to reveal the deep mysteries to one person that no one else is privy to, yet He has not told them to submit?" This is what it really takes for you to bring your supply in a harmonious way. If you don't recognize these attributes in yourself, you're going to struggle.

Chapter Thirteen:
The Art of Standards

In today's church, it is amazing to me how many men you will see that are effeminate. *Effeminate* means "to have a very feminine demeanor." You'll be shocked to see how many male pastors and praise and worship leaders/members have very feminine ways about them. It's beginning to change in terms of leadership and headship. One of the signs of the Jezebel spirit is that people begin to blur the line of identity in terms of their sexuality. Women will become more masculine and men will become more feminine. So in order for Satan to be successful, he must blur the line.

There are people who I came up in the ministry with that have come to the decision they're not going to wear a suit and tie anymore. Now, I do not care what you wear, that's your decision. Here's what I believe, I feel that I'm responsible for the office in which I occupy. If the President of the United States decides that he should be wearing a suit, then I'm going to do the same thing. In my opinion, the office in which I stand and the responsibility which has been placed upon me is equally as important. So if he deems that by his office he should carry himself a certain way, then I deem by the office in which I stand, I should do the same thing. That's where I'm at and I'm not backing up on it and I do not care what people think. "Well, that's not relevant." I don't care; you won't see me in a Hawaiian t-shirt and a pair of khakis telling you that we're all okay. I have a responsibility to maintain the position in which I was given.

Now you can certainly choose for yourself, but here's my point. When you start seeing people backing up on how they dress and all of a sudden the church has become so casual, everything becomes casual. What happened to raising the standard and setting the bar? The Bible says that when the enemy comes in like a flood that God raises the standard. Why do we need to raise the standard?

The standard should be set at a level in which is higher than what everybody's expectation is. Does God really care if you call your leader "pastor?" Well, I think that it's not about whether God cares in as much as it is about you discerning the role that a person plays in your life. I have seen congregation members calling their pastors by the first name. All of a sudden its "Hey Dave!" How are you doing? Dave can't do anything for you. I might not even like Dave, but Pastor Dave can do something for me. Pastor Dave has an office in which he stands and by the virtue and necessity of the office, and the anointing that comes with the office alone is why I need him. Titles alone are not important what is important is that you recognize the office in which someone stands. I think that the name game has gone to the extreme where everyone is a bishop, prophet, or apostle. However it still stands that we should recognize the office and not allow ourselves to back up and lower the bar.

In this effeminate male problem that we are experiencing, we are starting to see it in praise and worship and pulpit ministry. Now we are seeing that in some male Christian artists. They're very good musically; they're even very gifted musically, but there always seems to be a tinge of femininity in some. Satan was God's praise and worship leader. That's why people in praise and worship have to be very careful that they don't think that the applause and the worship is for them. That's what happened to Satan. He led worship and then all of a sudden he started believing too heavily in himself. The

Congregation loves God. Sometimes these praise and worship people want to be about themselves. If they are not careful they start believing their own press, or as my grandmother used to say, they start smelling themselves!

Careful not to get to a place where you start thinking, "Wait a minute, maybe all of this applause is for me." When Jesus came riding in on the donkey, I wonder with all the "Hosanna! Hosanna!" and the hoopla did the donkey start thinking that some of that applause was for him? No, they don't like you, they like the Christ riding on you. You just happen to be the vehicle at the time by which God is showing himself strong. We have to be careful to be the stage, not try to be on stage.

But my point is that music is an influence in the world. Satan seeks to have a stronghold in the area of music because he can influence people greatly. As a child, when you were taught your ABC's, it was set to music so that you would learn them quickly. Why did they set it to music? Music is an enhancer to help retain knowledge, not necessarily truth. Not all knowledge is truth.

You see these things starting to happen in society and it's really starting to permeate into the church. Life begins to imitate art. Why? People see it on TV and think that it's okay to live this way. To have an alternative lifestyle has become the norm. The challenge is that the Bible does not agree with that.

I'm about sick of all the Christian Reich, who continue to point out homosexuality but don't point out the rest of sin. I have a problem with that because once you start throwing stones and you live in a glass house, we have problems. It's all a problem for God. He did not alienate one issue and say, "This is a problem and this one isn't." There's no grading when it comes to sin; sin is sin. We have a unique position and challenge that we're dealing with but how did we blur the line? We blurred the line by blurring the characteristics and blurring the traits.

Listen, I'm not promoting hate, isolation or alienation. I want you to wake up. When you're clapping your hands and praising God and if you can't look at their face or behavior and tell whether or not they were a male or a female, you need to be very careful. You need to be paying attention because the lines are getting blurred in order to destroy the church's power.

I'm not backing up on how I dress because I'm not blurring that line. It's just the line that I've decided I refuse to blur. There are things that people will do and ask, "Well how come you won't do it?" It may not be illegal; it may not be immoral, but I just will not do it. I will not do it because it's a standard in which I've set. The Bible says that when the enemy comes in like a flood, the first thing God does is raise the standard because the enemy cannot live to the standard. All he can do is cause you to drop yours. If he can get you to drop your standard, then you cannot stay above the flood which means you get consumed by the flood. But if you understand how God functions and how God works, He knows that Satan can only do but so much. This is why people are stuck in attack. They're wondering, "Why do I keep going through this attack?" You won't raise your standards.

Going to church is a standard for me. That's not an option, not even a discussion. I do not even wake up and go, "Do I want to go to church today?" This is what I do; this is who I am.

People do not treat God with the honor that He respects, expects, and requires. They wonder why they're struggling. It does not make any sense to me, but yet I see it all the time. People will not honor God until all hell breaks loose in their lives. The word *Jezebel* means, "Without head, without leadership." It's not exclusive to females, it can also be a male that will struggle with the spirit of Jezebel. They don't want to be in submission, they don't want to be told what to do. It happens everywhere. It happens in the workplace and it happens in the home.

You ever hear that saying, "If mama ain't happy nobody is happy?" You know that's straight from the pit of hell don't you? What do you mean "If mama ain't happy?" How about Dad? Dad doesn't count? How about if both of them aren't happy? See, and people run around saying that stuff. It's demonic; it's Jezebel. You mean to tell me we're going to disrupt the entire family because mama ain't happy? What, did Dad die? In my humble opinion if momma ain't happy then she just ain't happy. She ought to get happy. It is bizarre to me how we have accepted this rhetoric as gospel when it is straight out of the pit of hell. Should we want mama to be happy? Absolutely, and mama should be responsible for daddy's happiness, as well. It should be equitable. When all this is done and settled, God isn't going to look just at mama. He's going to hold daddy responsible for his family.

There is nothing biblical that says, "As long as you made mama happy, everything is right with God in your family." It tells us to submit one to another. There's a responsibility that tells us to love our wives, and wives to respect and honor her husband. Then everything goes well. This is important because the only way Jezebel can survive is when you have anAhab.

An Ahab is the one running around saying, "If mama ain't happy, nobody's happy." You've been hoodwinked, bamboozled, run amuck, deceived, shanghaied. That needs to stop because that's what allows Jezebel to function, the man who won't step into his office and say, "No, we knocking that off. We are going to church today; that's what we fitting to do. As for me and my house..." Joshua did not say, "Honey, what's our house going to do today?" He said, "For as me and my house we're going to serve the Lord." I am not promoting a chauvinistic viewpoint. What I am saying is that the men need to step up.

THE ART OF FOLLOWING

Chapter Fourteen:
The Art of Order

"Miriam and Aaron talked against Moses behind his back because of his Cushite wife (he had married a Cushite woman)…"
- Numbers 12:1 MSG

A Cush woman was from Ethiopia. If we could put it in today's language, they had a problem with Moses marrying this little black girl. Miriam and Aaron are talking against Moses and it amazes me that they felt it necessary to speak against whom the leader was pursuing. It was none of their business. If he was not preaching the truth, preaching the gospel or you're not getting fed, let's discuss it. But in terms of what Moses was doing in his personal life it was not their place. God began to speak to them because they were murmuring against him.

"And they said, Hath the Lord indeed spoken not only by Moses? Hath he not spoken also by us? And the Lord heard it."
- Numbers 12:2 KJV

It's amazing to me how they felt that they could hear from God too. "We have the anointing too!" The problem is that they had it two, but they were not number one.

(Now the man Moses was very meek, above all the men which were upon the face of the earth.) And the Lord spake unto Moses, and unto Aaron, and unto Miriam, Come out ye three unto the tabernacle of the congregation. And they three came out. And the Lord came down in the pillar of the cloud, and stood in the door of the tabernacle, and called Aaron and Miriam: and they both came forth. And he said, Hear now my words: If there be a prophet among you, I the Lord will make myself known unto him in a vision, and will speak unto him in a dream.
- Numbers 12: 3-6 KJV

They are complaining about Moses and God heard it. God calls them all outside and said, "If there be a prophet among you, I will make myself known unto him in a vision and in a dream." My servant Moses is not, so who is faithful in all my house. With him will I speak mouth to mouth, even apparently. Not in dark speeches and the similitude of the Lord shall behold. Wherefore then were ye not afraid to speak against my servant Moses?"

He called them prophets. Now was Moses a prophet? He was, but Moses was also the shepherd. There are some doctrines that are trying to get people to believe that the prophet and the apostles are the ones leading every church. Further, they believe that the prophet has to run the house. In the local church, there is no office higher than the office of the shepherd. In other words, God was letting them know that he gave Moses insight with his eyesight. Not just visions and dreams but he speaks to him mouth to mouth.

Moses was the shepherd. He was the leader of God's people. That's what made him different. You have people that think the prophets are coming only to bring correction to the church. No, what the prophets will do is reveal the mind of God and that may, at times bring correction. The local church is under the headship of Christ as the Chief Shepherd and the pastors as the under-shepherds. That's why in the local church there is no higher office than the office of a shepherd. People try to come into our church and they're like, "I'm a prophet and a prophetess." I don't care if you are a "prophe-mess", in this house there is no higher office than the shepherd.

When I go and preach at other churches, I submit myself to that pastor. I will ask that pastor what they would like me to teach. If they want me to lay hands on people. What do they want me to do. Of course, I hear from God, but God is not going to send me somewhere to disrupt another man's house particularly if that man is not submitted to my authority.

Aaron and Miriam did not qualify to bring correction to Moses. Did Moses ever get corrected? Yes, but who did it? His father-in-law, Jethro. Moses was trying to do everything himself, so God needed to bring correction to Moses and he used his father-in-law, Jethro. Jethro was someone who Moses went to tend sheep for, someone who was in a higher position of authority, in his life. If you don't qualify to bring correction than seek out someone who does, and pray that the one who does qualify is able to correct that person and help them make the adjustments. But God doesn't adjust up from the sheep to the shepherd. Your church would be going crazy by direction if the pastor had to heed every opinion. Notice I did not say 'counsel' or 'advice', I said 'opinion'. You know what they say about opinions.

Moses was not corrected by Miriam and Aaron although they were prophets. I love how God said, "If there be a prophet among you...." The tonality of that is almost like, "If you even were one, what are you thinking? If you really were a prophet, you'd know better." In that, I want you to see something. They did not qualify. On a side note, Miriam ended up with leprosy for a period of time.

You have people that say things like, "They're one of those 'Don't touch God's anointed' types of churches...," and they make fun of that. There is a proper way to handle things. If you feel that something is taught incorrectly or going wrong in error, there's a way to handle that. But if you're coming into a place with the wrong attitude just to disrupt, distract, derail and destroy then you'd better pay attention to not touching God's anointed. That's not a joke; that's a real thing. You're better off praying until something happens. Maybe it's your clarity that needs to change. Maybe it's your revelation that needs to come up. You never know. If there's a problem, there's nothing wrong with making a problem known to the appropriate people. Maybe there are things that need to be dealt with, but sometimes people can get all super righteous and cause major damage.

A spirit of Jezebel doesn't care because she's not trying to bring correction, she's trying to destroy. She flutters about in speaking into ears drawing people unto herself. You know, somebody can't be seen by the pastor and the first thing she does is go to them and say things like, "You know I care about you. I'll go to lunch with you. I love you; I don't know what's wrong with Pastor, he's just too busy!"

"And the anger of the Lord was kindled against them; and he departed. And the cloud departed from off the tabernacle; and, behold, Miriam became leprous, white as snow: and Aaron looked upon Miriam and, behold, she was leprous. And Aaron said unto Moses, Alas, my Lord, I beseech thee, lay not the sin upon us, wherein we have done foolishly, and wherein we have sinned. Let her not be as one dead, of whom the flesh is half consumed when he cometh out of his mother's womb. And Moses cried unto the Lord, saying, Heal her now, O God, I beseech thee. And the Lord said unto Moses, If her father had but spit in her face, she should not be ashamed seven days? let her be shut out from the camp seven days, and after that let her be received in again. And Miriam was shut out from the camp seven days: and the people journeyed not till Miriam was brought in again. And afterward the people removed from Hazeroth, and pitched in the wilderness of Paran."
- Numbers 12:9-16

Notice how Moses responded even though he was under attack with criticism. Even though they came against him he still was trying to intercede for them. It's by nature of the office in which the pastor stands. Even when people come against them, a pastor still wants the best for them. I can't tell you how many times people have done me wrong and knew that they were wrong. Yet when their life went to hell, which it usually does, they call me and the first thing I do is help.

"But what I do, that I will do, that I may cut off occasion from them which desire occasion; that wherein they glory, they may be found even as we. For such are false apostles, deceitful workers, transforming themselves into apostles of Christ. And no marvel; for Satan himself transformed into an angel of light. Therefore it is no great thing if his ministers also be transformed as the ministers of righteousness; whose end shall be according to their works."
- 2 Corinthians 11:12-15

There are going to be wolves that will rise up and say that they're sent by God. They're even going to demonstrate what appears to be an anointing. He said, "…it's no marvel…" In other words, Paul said it doesn't shock him because Satan can transform himself into an angel of light.

When people come to an organization without submitting to headship, that's how you can tell. I do not care if they're doing miracles or not, are you submitted somewhere? The presence of the supernatural is not the sole indication of the genuine anointing. I want to know do you have a pastor? If you don't have one, sorry; you will not preach here, plain and simple. You have to be submitted to a supply because it's the way God ordained it.

You have to be very careful with people that always say they have revelation, but cannot handle the basics. They do not tithe or attend a church, yet somehow, God revealed to them the fivefold, manifold wisdom of His grace and the depths of his unspeakable and unforetold mysteries. Still, they will not tithe. God did not tell them to submit, but he revealed all the deep things. They do not go to church, but they have revelation and light. Satan transformed himself into an angel of light. All revelation is not God revelation, and people who operate in the gifts have to be very careful because they can be ministered to by familiar spirits.

"Wherefore I take you to record this day, that I am pure from the blood of all men. For I have not shunned to declare to you all the counsel of God. Take heed therefore unto yourselves, and to all the flock, over which the Holy Ghost hath made you overseers, to feed the church of God which he hath purchased with his own blood."
- Acts 20:26-28

Now let me ask you a question; who's he talking to? He's talking not to just those in the church; he's talking about the overseers, the leaders. He didn't say they'll come in from the sheep fold, He said they'll come in among the leaders. Satan specifically chose Judas because he was in leadership. Leaders can have the greatest effect. "… for I know this that after my departing that grievous wolves enter in among you not sparing the flock. Also of your own selves shall men arise, speaking perverse things to draw disciples after them…"

When David commanded Joab not to kill Absalom, David was trying not to split the kingdom. Joab wanted to, and eventually did it anyway because he did not care. David wanted to spare the flock and Joab wanted his version of justice. You have to understand the difference between a pastor, (the shepherd) and the other offices. The pastor will tolerate some things because he's trying to spare the whole flock. He said, "…of your own selves shall men arise, speaking perverse things to draw people to themselves." Notice when you come against the Word, it draws people to you. When you are staying with the Word, they are repelled. Worldly people want the perverse things because that's what draws them. They're not drawing people to God they're drawing people unto themselves.

"And it came to pass after this, that Absalom prepared him chariots and horses, and fifty men to run before him. And Absalom rose up early, and stood beside the way of the gate: and it was so, that when any man that had a controversy came to the king for judgment, then Absalom called unto him, and said, Of what city art thou? And he said, Thy servant is of one of the tribes of Israel. And Absalom said unto him, See, thy matters are good and right; but there is no man deputed of the king to hear thee. Absalom said moreover, Oh that I were made judge in the land, that every man which hath any suit or cause might come unto me, and I would do him justice!"
- 2 Samuel 15:1-4

Absalom is catching people as they're coming to the king. The Bible tells us that Absalom was a very attractive man. The Bible also tells us that Satan was beautiful. Most think of Satan as this gnarly creature with horns and a pitchfork. He's not. If he showed up that way you'd know what he was and you'd be able to deal with it or run. Satan doesn't show up in that gnarly form that you see in all the scary movies. Satan shows up sometimes as your mother, your child, your spouse or your best friend. He doesn't show up foaming at the mouth.

Absalom was the most handsome man around. He had a nice chariot and fifty men to run before him. (Talk about making an entrance with an entourage!) If you're going to do it, that's how to do it. He stands before the people, catches them on the way to the king and intercepts their grievances. It's a spirit that elevates itself into a position it was never given. While David was trying desperately to steal the heart of God, Absalom was trying to steal the hearts of the people. Everything he heard, he responded with support and agreement even if it was wrong. The king never heard anything about it.

Be careful of people who intercept you when you're on your way to speak to your shepherd. They want to hear your matters. They're good at it. They'll call you because they see the look on your face at church. They're the ones that call and say, "Hey, how you doing? Oh, I just saw you. You know, you look as if you could use some prayer. I really want to be there for you. How are you doing?" It's a setup to intercept and intercede.

We've even had people at times that think their job was to protect the sheep from me. They thought that I was harsh, and sometimes I am. I can't be moved in tears all the time and I know that, at times, I will have to mourn with those who mourn. I also have insight with my eyesight and know when to instill faith. If you had a leader that was as shook up as you were you, both would get depressed and quit together.

I hate when I am at Starbucks in a counseling session, particularly with a female, and God starts reading their mail. All of a sudden, there's this large, African-American guy sitting across the table from this frail woman, regardless of the ethnicity, and she is bawling. In plain view of all the customers sitting at the surrounding tables, I appear to be somebody who has beaten her or broke up with her. I couldn't be counseling or helping her, nor giving her what God's told me to. People looking at me as if they're saying, "Meany!" I'm serious. Other people can have eyesight, but that doesn't mean they have insight.

What an Absolom will do is they come subtly. They can spot the ones that are having a bad day and so when you go over to the food table they just happen to be there. "Hey! How you doing? You doing alright? The Lord put you on my heart." Famous words; trust me. All

Absalom wanted to do was steal the hearts of the people. You've got to be careful because that's how church splits can happen.

Somebody charismatic with the gift of leadership begins to start wooing people. They stay after a little late and they just hop around, fluttering from one person to the next. They're propagating their ideas, seeking consensus. I'm giving my life for the sheep and you're going to protect them from me? Sometimes people have eyesight and no insight.

My response cannot always be, "Let's cry together." Sometimes my response has to be, "You know what? Seriously, suck them tears up. We are going to get in faith to fight this thing. We are not going to give in, shrink back, or sit here and cry. Crying is over!" Sometimes that's what people need. There are times where I will sob with people for a little bit, but that's not always the best resolution.

Absolom had natural eyesight, so he picked the ones who looked troubled. Absolom looked the part, dressed the part and acted the part. Jezebel's spirit doesn't have the anointing so the only way for it to appear to have an anointing is it must imitate, not duplicate.

When you have spiritual children, you're depositing wisdom into their life and you're trying to duplicate. However, since Jezebel is not submitted to that, the only thing it can do is imitate. They can get fifty men to run before their beautiful chariot; they can dress the part, they can look handsome, but they will not have the anointing. That's why Paul said they come as ministers of light. They can look the part and they can talk the part; have all the "Christianese" down, but there is no anointing. That's why Jezebel has to get close and imitate your behavior. Then, because it acts like you, you find favor with it because you say, "Hey, it's like me!" But it is not there for any other purpose but to steal, kill and destroy.

You can see these characteristics because success always leaves clues, but so does betrayal. When you're watching people in your life, watch them. Take a moment to observe them, to observe yourself and say, "Why do I feel this way? Why do I even think like this? Why do I have such a problem with this?"

I had a conversation with somebody not too long ago in which I asked them, "Why is this an issue for you?" Their response was, "I feel hypocritical because it has nothing to do with me; it's none of my business, but I just can't get over it." How do we allow Satan to derail us without cause why? People who have been in church for years and should know better, they've taught fifty million times, yet and still Satan can wind them up very quickly. Those of you who are single don't you ever date somebody who just came into Christ or is not in Christ yet. Let me tell you why.

If they're on the edge, it doesn't take much to knock them off. If you want to date her, her heart better be so hid in Christ that you'll have to chase Him to find her. Vice versa, you want to date him? Don't date him because he has the fifty men running in front of his chariot or because he has a nice chariot. Make sure he has a nice one, but don't date him because he has one. He should be a man of means! However, that's not the deciding factor because Satan will disguise himself to make you think, "Maybe I'm safe with confiding my information in them and bringing them into my life." Let me tell you something, the end of it is destruction. You ought to be happy that God moved people out of your life. It might have been painful for you, but you should be happy. You should be shouting, "THANK YOU GOD!" Because if God hadn't moved them now, could you imagine what you would have had to go through?

"And as they did eat, he said, Verily I say unto you, that one of you shall betray me. And they were exceeding sorrowful, and began every one of them to say unto him, Lord, is it I?"
- Matthew 26: 21-22

Jesus knew who was going to betray him, but he said to them, "One of you is going to betray me." Their answer wasn't, "Hey, you know I've been watching Judas man, Judas been acting kinda shady...." Peter did not say, "You know what? John is always running around talking about how Jesus loves him as if he doesn't love everybody else. I bet you its John!" None of them went down that road. They all said, "Is it I?" That meant that, among them, they could not discern who it was. So the ultimate question had to be, "Is it me?" They esteemed each other better than themselves, and they were circumspect about their own life. When you talk about difficult subjects such as this, people will get offended.

Here's your question;

"Is it I?"

What if it is you? You may not want to deal with it or look at it. You may want to turn your back on it, but if it's derailing you from the plan that God has for you, then there's a point where you've got to say, "Is it I?" If it is me, I want to make the adjustment. I want to turn from it and keep progressing in the things of God because there's a plan and a purpose in God. There's a future in God, there's a destiny in God and I don't have time to travel down a wrong road. Maybe I take inventory, and maybe I come back and say, "Hey, it isn't me." Great!

It's bizarre to me how they never began to accuse each other, but they became circumspect of themselves. You have to ask yourself, are you willing to be circumspect? Are you willing to be honest about why you feel what you feel, why you think what you think and why you act the way you act?

Do you really have the elements and the forerunners of success in your life? Do you have the attitude of loyalty and commitment? Are you that person that can be depended upon; or do you always buck the system? I find the people in the church that are on top of their game. I see to it personally that they are developed and promoted. The ones that aren't ready, I leave them alone until they are ready. I'm not mad at them. They're just not ready yet. They are still a little pink in the middle and need more time in the oven. They need to cook a little while longer. I might turn it up 450 degrees and let them sit there for a minute until their ready because we all have a call to walk out, we have a mission and you can't build a church with punk.

Punk is wood that cannot be used to construct anything because it's rotten inside and out. It is used it to ignite various things.. It's easily combustible. Easily lit, but you can't build anything with it. If you're going to do anything great for God, you better learn how to get your flesh under control. If you cannot control yourself, you'll be running around looking for the Ahab. You'll jump from church to church until you find the one pastor who will let you do what you want to do. You will not know that's what you're looking for, but that's really it. You're looking for the one who'll side with you, pat you on the head and agree with you. Now you have come to the smorgasbord of life and you've picked only the food you wanted to eat. All the while, your veggies, have been ignored.

"Is it I Lord?"

Other Featured Titles

Welcome to the Teaching Ministry of Rev. Gene Herndon, Senior Pastor of Stonepoint Community Church! For almost ten years, he has been providing simple, practical teaching and understanding of the Bible. Our mission is to inspire, improve and help you shape your future into nothing short of the best of what God has for you! Gene Herndon Ministries is committed to bringing the truth of God's word to you in an authentic, practical, humorous and easy to apply way.

identity - Discover Your Authority in Christ

Many times as Christians, we do not realize that our conditions of life are not always our position. When we study the Word of God it is clear about who it says we are, what God says we can have, and what God truly says we can do. It is a must for every believer to understand who they are in Christ positionally, spiritually, and naturally. This book will help you discover who you are in Christ positionally so that by using your authority, you may change your life condition.

$12.99 (One Book)

Betrayal - Learning To Trust Again

Betrayal is the breaking of trust and confidence. Betrayal is often the focal point of a good movie or book but in real life it can be devastating. Not only in terms of personal relationships, friendships, and marriages but also by the church. This book will help you to begin the healing process and to quickly create healthy boundaries in your life.

$9.99 (One Book)

Getting Out of the Wilderness

God has given us many promises and the Bible tells us that the promises of God are Yes and Amen! This powerful book reveals the limiting thoughts, beliefs, and ideas that keep the believer from possessing whatever God has promised you. You will be forced to face your fears and stretch the limits set by your self imposed boundaries. This book will help you to acquire new insight to rid our-selves of the subtleties of poverty thinking that can hinder and often destroy the prosperity of God in our lives.

$9.99 (One Book)

And remember, in all you're getting, get understanding!

231

Made in the USA
Middletown, DE
06 February 2021

33075277R00136